Russian Nouns
of Common Gender
in Use

Russian Nouns of Common Gender in Use is a unique collection of more than 150 nouns that mainly have grammatical features of the feminine gender, but refer to both male and female persons.

This book provides the meanings of the words and explains their use in discourse with the help of examples from literature, media, and everyday speech. Each entry includes parallel English translations, which are analogous and appropriate to the given context. These enable the reader to easily grasp each word's organic place and purpose in a particular sentence or situation.

This book will serve as a valuable tool for students and instructors, translators, scholars, and anyone interested in learning the Russian language.

Marina Rojavin is teaching at Bryn Mawr College. She specializes in Russian language and culture, Soviet film and, in particular, character archetypes in Soviet cinema of the 60s–80s; Russian media studies; Russian intellectuals in Imperial Russia; and Russian intelligentsia. Marina has published articles on the semantic category of gender in Russian and Ukrainian and on the grammatical category of gender in Russian. She and Allan Reid published *A Guide to Russian Words and Expressions that Cause Difficulties* in 2004. Her most recent publications are the textbook *Russian for Advanced Students* (2013), completed with her colleagues, and the volume *Women in Soviet Film: The Thaw and Post-Thaw Periods* (2017), edited together with Timothy Harte (Bryn Mawr College).

Alexander Rojavin is currently in law school, studying international law and public policy. A native speaker of English and Russian, he has focused his undergraduate and graduate studies on Soviet and post-Soviet media space, producing a master's thesis on media ownership in Ukraine and on the legal framework within which the Ukrainian media operates. Alexander helped translate a series of theater treatises for Nikolai Demidov's *Becoming an Actor-Creator* (2016). He has also translated a series of contemporary Russian plays (forthcoming) and a work of creative nonfiction by Yevsey Tseytlin, *Long Conversations in Anticipation of a Joyous Death* (2018), which grapples with the history and fate of Lithuania's Jewry.

Russian Nouns of Common Gender in Use

Marina Rojavin
and Alexander Rojavin

LONDON AND NEW YORK

First published 2019
by Routledge
2 Park Square, Milton Park, Abingdon, Oxon OX14 4RN

and by Routledge
52 Vanderbilt Avenue, New York, NY 10017

Routledge is an imprint of the Taylor & Francis Group, an informa business

© 2019 Marina Rojavin and Alexander Rojavin

The right of Marina Rojavin and Alexander Rojavin to be identified as authors of this work has been asserted by them in accordance with sections 77 and 78 of the Copyright, Designs and Patents Act 1988.

All rights reserved. No part of this book may be reprinted or reproduced or utilised in any form or by any electronic, mechanical, or other means, now known or hereafter invented, including photocopying and recording, or in any information storage or retrieval system, without permission in writing from the publishers.

Trademark notice: Product or corporate names may be trademarks or registered trademarks, and are used only for identification and explanation without intent to infringe.

British Library Cataloguing-in-Publication Data
A catalogue record for this book is available from the British Library

Library of Congress Cataloging-in-Publication Data
Names: Rojavin, Marina, author. | Rojavin, Alexander, author.
Title: Russian nouns of common gender in use / Marina Rojavin and Alexander Rojavin.
Description: New York : Routledge, 2019. | Includes bibliographical references and index.
Identifiers: LCCN 2018046162 | ISBN 9781138483804 (hardback : alk. paper) | ISBN 9781138483828 (pbk. : alk. paper) | ISBN 9781351053815 (ebook)
Subjects: LCSH: Russian language—Noun—Glossaries, vocabularies, etc. | Russian language—Gender.
Classification: LCC PG2211 .R65 2019 | DDC 491.75—dc23
LC record available at https://lccn.loc.gov/2018046162

ISBN: 978-1-138-48380-4 (hbk)
ISBN: 978-1-138-48382-8 (pbk)
ISBN: 978-1-351-05381-5 (ebk)

Typeset in Times New Roman
by Apex CoVantage, LLC

Contents

About the book	vi
About Russian nouns of common gender	viii
Terminology	xi
Entries	1
Bibliography	118
List of Russian nouns of common gender	128

About the book

Russian Nouns of Common Gender in Use is a unique collection of 155 nouns. The main objective of this book is to illuminate the use of Russian words that are defined as nouns of common gender – nouns that have grammatical forms of the feminine gender, but can refer to either males or females. The book has features of both a reference book and a dictionary, and it concerns itself with the semantic analysis of these words, in addition to explaining the roles they have in sentences, their stylistic specifics, and their use in full context, with examples from literature, contemporary media, and everyday speech. Users of this book will develop a comprehension of how to use common gender nouns through discourse – specifically through certain verbal situations based not only on the underlying semantic meanings, but rather on the content of typical extra-linguistic life situations. This book would serve as a valuable tool for students and instructors, translators, scholars, and anyone interested in learning the Russian language.

The book consists of one main part (entries), in addition to introductory parts, and index (list of common gender nouns). This list does not contain translations into English, because the majority of these nouns do not have exact translations in light of their semantic peculiarities. Consequently, the main part, which contains the common gender nouns in alphabetical order, has detailed semantic analyses and descriptions of these words on a grammatical and stylistic basis.

Every entry includes an explanation of meanings, how the common gender word is used in specific contexts in combination with other words. Some entries include fixed phrases or sayings, synonyms and/

About the book　vii

or antonyms so that a reader can better comprehend the words' meaning. All entries include examples with English translations that are not literal, but analogous and appropriate to the given circumstances, enabling the reader to easily grasp each word's organic place and purpose in a particular sentence or situation. The translation of a number of words in examples may not be identical to the translation given in the description of the meaning and may instead be contextual synonyms. Examples are placed in chronological order – quotes from earlier sources appear first. Some words are not presented in the book because of the low frequency of their use in discourse or their archaism. Examples from literature and media have been taken from www.ruscorpora.ru/.

About Russian nouns of common gender

Nouns that belong to the common gender can refer to both males and females, even though they predominantly have grammatical features of the feminine gender, i.e. they have feminine endings **-а, -я**. Common gender nouns can be classified into the following groups:

1   Nouns that indicate personal characteristics and traits, in some cases with a pejorative implication: **вы́скочка** *parvenu*, **жа́дина** *greedy person*, **зану́да** *bore*, **зубри́ла** *rote memorizer*, **неве́жда** *ignoramus*, **неря́ха** *slob*, **пла́кса** *crybaby*, **подли́за** *brown noser*, **со́ня** *sleepyhead*.

2   A few nouns that designate physical peculiarities: **левша́** *left-hander*, **правша́** *right-hander*, **двойня́шка** *twin*, **тройня́шка** *triplet*, **кале́ка** *cripple*.

3   A few nouns that designate social status or someone's profession: **сирота́** *orphan*, **судья́** *judge*, **колле́га** *colleague*.

4   Diminutive first names that can refer to both males and females: **Са́ша, Шу́ра** (Алекса́ндр/Алекса́ндра), **Же́ня** (Евге́ний/Евге́ния), **Ва́ля** (Валенти́н/Валенти́на), **Па́ша** (Па́вел/Поли́на or Праско́вья), **Сла́ва** (Вячесла́в, Миросла́в, Мстисла́в, Яросла́в/Миросла́ва, Яросла́ва), **Вале́ра** (Вале́рий/Вале́рия), **Стёпа** (Степа́н, Степани́да).

5   Last names of foreign origin, as well as a number of last names with endings other than **-а, -я**: **Ки́ржнер, Ро́зенберг, Степане́нко, Петре́нко, Жива́го, Черны́х, Петро́вых.**

6   Some indeclinable nouns of foreign origin with endings other than **-а, -я** may also be considered to be of common gender.

About Russian nouns of common gender ix

This group includes nouns that name persons of both biological genders: **инкóгнито** *incognito*, **протежé** *protégé*, **парвеню́** *parvenu*, and nouns that can refer to animals of both biological genders: **шимпанзé** *chimpanzee*, **кенгурý** *kangaroo*.

Many nouns of all three genders can be used to refer to either males or females. However, unlike nouns of common gender, which have a dual gender by default, other nouns can only be either masculine (e.g. **дирéктор** *director*), feminine (e.g. **знаменúтость** *celebrity*), or neuter (e.g. **лицó** *face*).

Many nouns of different genders are commonly used to refer to both sexes and metaphorically indicate certain characteristics, as for example **тря́пка** *rag*, **пень** *stump*, **змея́/змею́ка** *snake*, **дуб** *oak*, **юлá** *spinning top,* and many others. However, they belong to a specific grammatical gender and agree with other nouns according to their gender.

Because the semantics of nouns from the fourth and fifth groups are straightforward, this book focuses on nouns from the other groups, primarily those from the first group, which does not distinguish biological sex without context or else semantic or syntactic associations with modifying words that might imply belonging to the biological sex. Biological sex is actualized in speech in each specific situation, individual context, or set of circumstances. The personal pronouns **онá** or **он** and first names, full or short, e.g. **Елéна (Лéна), Андрéй (Андрю́ша)** (except the short forms of names that belong to group 4), are the main indicators of the referred person's sex – they replace common gender nouns according to the actual biological sex of their referee.

Common gender nouns may play different roles in a sentence. The grammatical gender of the parts of speech that modify common gender nouns, including adjectives, pronominal adjectives, verbs, and participles, may vary. The biological sex of the referred person might be explicated by the forms of words that syntactically concur with the common gender noun. In the nominative case, nouns may combine with adjectives and possessive pronouns of either masculine or feminine gender. In sentences with a common gender noun as a subject, a predicate in the past tense can be masculine and refer to a male, although the feminine gender agreement does not show the referee's sex. For example, in the sentence **Э́тот сóня проспáл из-за**

x *About Russian nouns of common gender*

сло́манного буди́льника. *That sleepyhead overslept because of a broken alarm*, the past tense verb **проспа́л** shows that **со́ня** refers to a male person. On the other hand, a sentence with an agreement like **Э́та со́ня проспала́ из-за сло́манного буди́льника.** *That sleepyhead slept through the alarm*, where the demonstrative pronoun **э́та** and the past tense verb **проспала́** formally indicate the feminine gender, do not prove that the referred person is female, and more extended context is needed to ascertain the referred individual's sex. In cases when a common gender noun in the nominative case is a part of a compound predicate and refers to the subject, the verbal part of the predicate shows the sex of the referee, like in the sentence **Я был/была́ така́я худы́шка.** *I used to be so thin.*

When these nouns are used in cases other than the nominative, they tend to take on feminine agreement regardless of the biological sex of the referenced person (the subject), although the masculine gender can also be used when referring to males. **Пётр ста́л ужа́сной/ ужа́сным жа́диной.** *Pyotr has become a terrible cheapskate.* When a common gender noun functions as an object and does not refer to a subject, the biological sex of the referee might be shown by the forms of other words or in more extended context. In the sentence **Она́ ходи́ла с э́той раззя́вой к нота́риусу.** *She went to the notary public with that scatterbrain*, the sex of the person denoted by the noun **раззя́вой** is not explicit and more information is needed, such as the name of the referee. It should be noted that some nouns are often better paired with pronouns of a specific gender. For example, **к э́тому ехи́дине** *to that snake*, **с э́той чертя́кой** *with that devil* is not good, because the nouns **ехи́дина** and **чертя́ка** tend to refer more often to females and males respectively.

Terminology

Appositive
A nominal or a nominal phrase that clarifies and follows another nominal (a word or group of words that function as a noun).

Colloquial language
Used in conversations in an informal way. It is opposed to formal language.

Contemporary language
The language norm accepted since the second half of the 20th century.

Elevated style
Used in writing and speech that is considered dignified or sophisticated.

Formal language
Used in formal situations. Utilizes proper grammar and syntax, not employing colloquialisms or slang. It is opposed to informal language.

Informal language
Used in informal situations. Utilizes colloquialisms or slang. It is opposed to formal language.

Language styles
Includes formal, informal, colloquial, neutral, and elevated.

xii *Terminology*

Neutral style
Without stylistic color. It is opposed to colloquial, elevated, and bookish styles.

Object
Indicates someone or something and answers the questions of oblique cases. Objects that relate to transitive verbs are direct objects, and they are used in the accusative case.

Phrase
A group of words that functions as a grammatically acceptable constituent.

Predicate
Conveys what the subject does, did, will do, or would do to or with something, or what/who the subject is. The predicate always is a word or word group that acts as a verb.

Pronominal
Functions as a pronoun.

Subject
The main part of a sentence, connected to a predicate; it is the doer of an action in a sentence. It answers questions of the nominative case **кто?** *who?*, **что?** *what?*

Entries

Аферю́га

A swindler; someone who engages in con artistry. Expresses strong disapproval and contempt.

Originates from the noun **афери́ст** *swindler*, which is synonymous, but **аферю́га** is more emphatic, though used less frequently. Can be synonymous with **авантюри́ст** *opportunist*. Semantically close to **деля́га**, **жу́лик** *cheat*, **прощелы́га**. Can be associated with the noun **вор** *thief*.

See **деля́га**, **прощелы́га**.

Вот, – говорю́, – това́рищ капита́н, пойма́ли аферю́гу, кото́рый бума́жники оставля́ет с пятьюста́ми ты́сячами, а пото́м че́стных люде́й гра́бит. (Л. Изма́йлов «Афери́сты» 1996)	"You see, captain," I say, "we caught the swindler who leaves wallets with five hundred thousand, cash, and then robs honest folk." (Izmaylov, *Swindlers*, 1996)
Ну что твоя́ аферю́га? Пообеща́ла миллио́ны и бы́стро исче́зла, прихвати́в твой кошелёк?	So, where's your little crook? She promises millions and then disappears with your wallet?
Е́сли кто-то про́сит предопла́ту, не ве́рьте – э́то аферю́га.	If somebody asks for advance pay, don't trust them – they're a crook.

2 *Entries*

Балабо́лка

A chatterbox. Someone who likes to talk a lot or gossip and who is bad at keeping secrets. Generally expresses disapproval, but can also convey more severe negative emotions.

Semantically close to **пустоме́ля**.

See пустоме́ля.

Но мне э́то ве́рный челове́к расска́зывал, не балабо́лка како́й-нибудь. (А. Саве́льев «Арка́н для букме́кера» 2000)	But I heard it from a reliable source, not from some chatterbox. (Savelyev, *A Lasso for the Bookmaker*, 2000)
Кварти́ра принадлежи́т мне, да́ча его́ сы́ну – вот э́той балабо́лке. (Э. Браги́нский, Э. Ряза́нов «Ти́хие о́муты» 2000)	The apartment belongs to me, the summer house to his son – to this chatterbox right here. (Braginsky & Ryazanov, *Still Waters*, 2000)
Я же не балабо́лка кака́я, разглаша́ть непрове́ренные фа́кты, – рыча́л генера́л. (В. Сини́цына «Му́за и генера́л» 2002)	"After all, I'm not some chatterbox, to divulge unproven facts," growled the general. (Sinitsyna, *The Muse and the General*, 2002)

Бедня́га (бедня́жка, бедня́жечка)

Someone who evokes compassion and sympathy. Expresses positive, sympathetic feelings. **Бедня́жка** and **бедня́жечка**, which have diminutive suffixes, express fondness.

Derived from the adjective **бе́дный** *poor*. Semantically close to **бедола́га** and **горемы́ка**.

See бедола́га, горемы́ка.

Ничего́ был па́рень Ви́тя. Спи́лся с го́ря, бедня́га. Поги́б в доро́жной катастро́фе. (И. Гре́кова «Фаза́н» 1984)	Vitya was a pretty good guy. Tried to drown his sorrows, poor thing. Died in a car crash. (Grekova, *The Peacock*, 1984)

Entries 3

Бедня́га так и не по́нял, что мир вокру́г живёт совсе́м по други́м зако́нам, жёстким и просты́м . . . (В. Пеле́вин «S.N.U.F.F.» 2011)

The poor guy never realized that the world around him lives according to a completely different set of rules – harsh and simple. (Pelevin, *S.N.U.F.F.*, 2011)

Пусть Ма́ша идёт отдыха́ть. Она́ же на нога́х не стои́т – бедня́га.

Masha should go rest. She's barely standing on her feet, poor thing.

Бедола́га

Someone who is miserable and pitiful. Conveys compassion or sympathy and articulates positive feelings.

Derived from the noun **беда́** *misfortune*. Semantically close to **бедня́га** and **горемы́ка**.

See **бедня́га**, **горемы́ка**.

Одна́жды э́тот бедола́га узна́л, что при коро́тком рукопожа́тии тре́буется эне́ргия, ра́вная ста ньюто́нам. (Ю. Бу́йда «Го́род палаче́й» // «Зна́мя» 2003)

Once, this poor sap found out that a short handshake requires a hundred Newtons' worth of energy. (Buida, "City of Executioners," 2003)

Как он, бедола́га тако́й, живёт с ней, не поня́тно.

It's unclear how he lives with her, the poor thing.

Ма́рья Анто́новна, бедола́га, до́лго боро́лась с невзго́дами.

Maria Antonovna, the poor thing, spent a long time battling various misfortunes.

Белору́чка

A slacker. Literally means **бе́лые ру́ки** *white hands*. Refers to someone who avoids physical work or other difficult, unpleasant, or dirty tasks. Conveys a negative attitude.

Can be a synonym for **безде́льник (безде́льница)** *idler*, **лентя́й (лентя́йка)** *lazybones*. Can also be synonymous with **чистоплю́й**

4 *Entries*

(**чистоплю́йка**) *sissy* when the person seeks to avoid the unpleasant facets of life in general. Can also be associated with the noun **не́женка**.

See **не́женка**.

Уж я тебя зна́ю, белору́чка ты э́такой! (И. Турге́нев «Хорь и Кали́ныч» 1847)	Oh, I know you well, you slacker! (Turgenev, *Hor' and Kalinych*, 1847)
Вы белору́чка, вы всегда́ на чужо́й счёт жи́ли, а мы с Мише́лем лю́ди рабо́тающие, вы нас заеда́ете. (Л. Андре́ев «Же́ртва» 1916)	You're a slacker, you've always lived off of someone else, while Michel and I are working people, and you feed off us. (Andreev, *The Sacrifice*, 1916)
– И горда́. А ру́ки мя́гкие, не́жные, белору́чка бу́дет. – Облома́ем, – отве́тил Пе́дро и углуби́лся в хозя́йственные счёты. (А. Беля́ев «Челове́к-амфи́бия» 1928)	"And so proud! But her hands are soft, tender – a slacker, this one." "We'll fix that," said Pedro and immersed himself in the activity accounts. (Belyaev, *Amphibian Man*, 1928)
А в том, что она́ не белору́чка, а работя́щая де́вушка, сознаю́щая свой долг и свои́ обя́занности, – в э́том, коне́чно, ба́бушка бы́стро разобра́лась. (А. Рыбако́в «Тяжёлый песо́к» 1978)	But grandma, of course, quickly picked up on the fact that she wasn't a slacker and was actually a hard-working girl, fully aware of her duty and responsibilities. (Rybakov, *Heavy Sand*, 1978)

Бродя́га (бродя́жка)

A tramp. A poor or homeless person; a jobless individual who wanders the world. Denotes a person who has no permanent residence and constantly travels from place to place. Can also refer to a person who simply loves to travel. Can express either positive or negative emotions. Usually refers to males. **Бродя́жка** is the diminutive form of the word, and it expresses fondness.

Derives from the verb **броди́ть** *to wander*. **Бездо́мный бродя́га** *homeless tramp* is a commonly used phrase. **Бродя́жка** can be a synonym for the feminine word **ни́щенка** *beggar woman*. Can be

Entries 5

combined with the adjectives **хитёр** and **силён** – **хитёр бродя́га** *oh, he's good!* and **силён бродя́га** *oh, he's good!* – to remark on someone's cunning or aptitude. Semantically close to **скита́лец** *vagabond.*

Это – полусумасше́дший бродя́га, безобра́зный и гру́бый мужи́к, эпиле́птик, ме́диум и юро́дивый. (И. А́нненский «Втора́я кни́га отраже́ний» 1909)

He's a half-mad tramp, an awful and barbaric man, an epileptic, a psychic, and a holy fool. (Annensky, *The Second Book of Reflections*, 1909)

Мы тепе́рь бу́дем всегда́ вме́сте, – говори́л ему́ во сне обо́рванный фило́соф-бродя́га, неизве́стно каки́м о́бразом вста́вший на доро́ге вса́дника с золоты́м копьём. (М. Булга́ков «Ма́стер и Маргари́та» 1966)

"We'll always be together now," the vagabond philosopher said to him in his sleep, having somehow appeared on the road before the rider with the golden spear. (Bulgakov, *Master and Margarita*, 1966)

По нату́ре бродя́га, альпини́ст, изобрета́тель но́вых риско́ванных ви́дов го́рного спо́рта, он в мо́лодости жил повсю́ду, болта́лся там и сям. (Д. Ру́бина «Бе́лая голу́бка Кордо́вы» 2009)

A vagabond by nature, an alpinist, an inventor of new and risky mountain sports, he spent his youth living everywhere, bumming from one place to another. (Rubina, *The White Dove of Cordoba*, 2009)

Оте́ц мой всю жизнь был бродя́гой и не сиде́л на ме́сте – его́ всегда́ тяну́ло к рюкзаку́.

My father was a wanderer his whole life and never stayed in one spot for long – he was always drawn to his backpack.

Брюзга́

A grouch. Someone who grumbles and complains constantly or who simply has an unbearable personality. Often refers to males. Conveys irritation.

Derives from the verb **брюзжа́ть** *to whine* and the noun **брюзжа́ние** *whining.* The adjectives **ве́чный** *eternal,* **ста́рый** *old,* and **несно́сный** *unbearable* are commonly used in combination with the noun.

6 *Entries*

Ли́чность замеча́тельная –
ма́стер на все ру́ки, но
хара́ктер преотвра́тный,
брюзга́, и, на́до сказа́ть, Петра́
Никола́евича он люби́л, но не
уважа́л ниско́лько. (Д. Гра́нин
«Иска́тели» 1954)

A fantastic individual – a
master of all trades, but he had
a horrible personality, he was a
grouch, and, it should be added,
he liked Pyotr Nikolaevich,
but didn't respect him at all.
(Granin, *The Searchers*, 1954)

Ты ужа́снейшая брюзга́ –
ве́чно всем не дово́лен.
Переста́нь ворча́ть.

You're a dreadful grouch –
you're always displeased
with everything. Stop your
grumbling.

С тако́й брюзго́й невозмо́жно
име́ть де́ло, она́ мо́жет
довести́ до бе́лого коле́ния.

It's impossible to have anything
to do with a grouch like her, she
can drive anyone up a wall.

Вообража́ла

Someone who thinks very highly of him or herself and shows off
profusely. Typically addresses girls who believe themselves to be
more beautiful than all others. Expresses disapproval.

Derived from the verb **вообража́ть** *to imagine*. Semantically close
to **задава́ка** and **зазна́йка**.

See **задава́ка**, **зазна́йка**.

Вообража́ла несча́стная!
Всё нос задира́ла, мол, оте́ц
её знамени́тый призови́к,
америка́нец. (А. Глади́лин
«Большо́й беговой день» 1983)

The miserable showoff! Her nose
was constantly in the air, as if to
say that her father was a famous
prize-getter, an American.
(Gladilin, *A Big Race Day*, 1983)

Костро́в всё-таки невероя́тный
вообража́ла, возомни́л себя́
чуть ли не Станисла́вским
и тре́бует от всех, чтобы
слу́шались его́, как бо́га.
(М. Ши́шкин «Вене́рин во́лос»
// «Зна́мя» 2005)

Kostrov is an unbelievable
showoff; he sees himself as
another Stanislavsky and
demands that everybody listen
to him as they would a god.
(Shishkin, "Venus's Hair,"
2005)

Нет, не сове́туется! Мо́жет
быть, зазна́йка, вообража́ла?

No, he doesn't ask for advice!
Could his head be that swollen?

Entries 7

Вро́де бы не до́лжен.
(В. Ро́зов «Удивле́ние пе́ред
жи́знью» 2014)

It shouldn't be. (Rozov, *A Surprise Before Life*, 2014)

Лю́ська настоя́щая
вообража́ла. Пе́ред
мальчи́шками всё вре́мя
красу́ется.

Lyus'ka is a real showoff. She's constantly preening before the boys.

Ворю́га

A thief or a crook. The same as **вор** *thief* and **воро́вка** *thief*, but **ворю́га** is more nuanced and emphatic, expressing more contempt and disrespect. However, it sounds less scornful than the feminine **воро́вка**; while **ворю́га** could be used teasingly – as, for example, **кот-ворю́га** *thieving cat* – **вор** and **воро́вка** would never be used in such a way.

Derived from the verb **ворова́ть** *to rob*.

В трамва́йной да́вке к нему́
подошёл опа́сный, о́пытный
ворю́га и зате́ял разгово́р.
(В. Гро́ссман «Жизнь и
судьба́» 1960)

A dangerous, grizzled crook approached him in the stampede of the tram and struck up a conversation. (Grossman, *Life and Fate*, 1960)

Никто́ тебя́ не зомби́ровал,
а был ты, я ви́жу, в про́шлой
жи́зни ворю́га после́дний!
(А. Слапо́вский «Синдро́м
Фе́никса» // «Зна́мя» 2006)

Nobody zombified you, but I can tell you were a damn thief in another life! (Slapovsky, "The Phoenix Syndrome," 2006)

Жу́лик он, ворю́га неуёмный.

He's a cheat, an insatiable thief.

Нача́льница на́ша – ворю́га и
взя́точница.

Our boss is a crook and a bribe-taker.

Вражи́на

An enemy. The same as **враг** *enemy*, but more emphatically scornful and disrespectful.

Он и есть лю́тая вражи́на,
неразоблачённая вражи́на,

He's a savage foe, the shrouded bastard. (Kabo, *October's*

8 *Entries*

вра́жеская мо́рда. (Л. Кабо́
«Рове́сники Октября́» 1964)

Contemporaries, 1964)

И подмыва́ло распра́виться
с ней, а не то что потака́ть
про́сьбам: кла́ссовая вражи́на,
по недосмо́тру ста́вшая
дире́ктором музе́я! (О. Во́лков
«Из воспомина́ний ста́рого
тенише́вца» 1988)

She was aching to destroy
her, not pander to her whims:
an enemy become museum
director because of an
oversight! (Volkov, *From
the Recollections of an Old
Tenishevets*, 1988)

Он не вражи́на. Он
революционе́р, но
крестья́нский, то есть
мелкобуржуа́зный.
(Ю. Три́фонов «Стари́к» 1978)

He wasn't an enemy. He was
a revolutionary, but a peasant,
or rather, petit bourgeoisie.
(Trifonov, *The Old Man*, 1978)

Проща́й, Усти́нов! Проща́й,
вражи́на моя́ бесконе́чная!
Бегу́ от тебя́! (С. Залы́гин
«Коми́ссия» 1976)

Farewell, Ustinov! Farewell,
my eternal foe! I flee from you!
(Zalygin, *The Commission*,
1976)

Вре́дина

An imp, a little devil. Someone who brings harm or does something
out of spite. Rather frequently used with regard to misbehaving children. Does not, however, convey a strong negative attitude.

Semantically close to **вре́дничать** *to cause mischief.*

Э́то ты намоли́ла, глаз наложи́ла.
Вот то́же кака́я вре́дина. А чего́
вре́дничать, спра́шивается?
(В. Личу́тин «Вдова́ Ню́ра» 1973)

This is all your praying – you
cursed us, you pain. Why must
you cause so much mischief?
(Lichutin, *The Widow Niura*, 1973)

Ко́стя, ты с ней не дружи́!
Она́ зна́ешь кака́я вре́дина!
(И. Пивова́рова «Мечта́ Ко́сти
Па́лкина» 1986)

Kostya, you don't want to be
friends with her! She's such a
little devil! (Pivovarova, *Kostya
Palkin's Dream*, 1986)

Ну и вре́дина же ты. Заче́м
де́лать то, что не про́сят?

You're such a pain in the ass.
Why do something that nobody
asked you to do?

Entries 9

Э́тот ребёнок ужа́сная
вре́дина – тако́й капри́зный!

This kid is a horrible pain – he's
so whiny!

Вруни́шка

A little liar. A diminutive form of **врун** *liar*. While the latter conveys
a negative attitude, **вруни́шка** can express fondness when addressing children, despite implying disapproval. Typically refers to children and males.

The synonymous **лгуни́шка** expresses the same emotions
as **вруни́шка**. Often used with the adjectives **ме́лкий** *little*,
стра́шный *terrible*, and **ужа́сный** *awful*.

See **лгуни́шка, хвастуни́шка**.

Я ду́маю, он вообще́
стра́шный вруни́шка,
болта́ет сам не зна́ет что.
(В. Нови́цкая «Безмяте́жные
го́ды» 1912)

I think he's a terrible little liar,
he makes things up that he
himself can't even make heads
or tails of. (Novitskaya, *The
Quiet Years*, 1912)

Па́вел Евгра́фович и не
по́мнил о ме́лком вруни́шке,
кото́рый бара́хтался как
мог, что́бы перекрути́ться
в суро́вой жи́зни.
(Ю. Три́фонов «Стари́к» 1978)

Pavel Evgrafivich didn't
even recall the little liar who
floundered as he could to
make it out of his rough
life. (Trifonov, *The Old Man*,
1978)

Кака́я же ты вруни́шка, На́стя,
ни одному́ сло́ву нельзя́
ве́рить.

You're such a little liar, Nastya,
you can't trust a single word
you say.

Сын её, хотя́ уже́ и взро́слый,
но тако́й же вруни́шка, как
был в де́тстве.

Even though her son has grown
up, he's still the same little liar
he was as a kid.

Всезна́йка

A know-it-all. This person confidently believes that he knows everything better than everyone else or pretends that he knows everything.
Often used with regard to children and young people. Carries a

10 *Entries*

negative connotation and sounds accusatory, but can also be neutral.

Derived from **всё знать** *to know everything.*

Свои́м умо́м бы не доду́мались. Э́то Анфи́м Ефи́мович, Ю́рочка, – всеве́д – всезна́йка. Про тебя́ слыха́л, про твоего́ отца́, де́душку моего́ зна́ет, всех, всех. (Б. Пастерна́к «До́ктор Жива́го» 1957)	"We'd never have figured it out. This is Anfim Yefimovich, Yurochka, he knows everything. He knows about you, about your father, he knows my grandfather, he knows everyone, everybody." (Pasternak, *Doctor Zhivago*, 1957)
Геро́й рома́на, суперме́н, краса́вец и всезна́йка, обречённый при э́том блужда́ть на задво́рках о́бщества, пока́ нетипи́чен для нема́ссовой ру́сской про́зы. («Парк культу́ры» // «Столи́ца» 1997)	The novel's protagonist is a good-looking superman who knows everything, but who is condemned to wander around the edge of society – not a typical character for small-scale Russian prose. ("Culture Park," 1997)
Алёна, ты невероя́тная всезна́йка. Отку́да ты всегда́ всё зна́ешь?	Alyona, you're an incredible know-it-all. How do you always know everything?
У твоего́ всезна́йки есть отве́ты на все вопро́сы.	Your know-it-all has an answer for every question.

Вы́жига

A cheapskate, a skinflint. Someone who refuses to spend a single cent more than he has to and tries to squeeze as much money out of every situation as possible. Expresses strong negative emotions. Often refers to males.

Semantically close to **жу́лик** *cheat*, **пройдо́ха**, and **прощелы́га**, but the closest is **сквалы́га**.

See **пройдо́ха, прощелы́га, сквалы́га**.

И не поду́майте, чтоб я был вы́жига како́й и́ли	And don't think that I was some kind skinflint or that I

жу́льничество с мое́й
стороны́, а про́сто из чувств!
(А. Че́хов «Сва́дьба» 1889)

dissembled – it was merely the
heat of passion! (Chekhov, *The
Wedding*, 1889)

Дя́дя То́ля вы́жига, покупа́ет
себе́ потихо́ньку бе́лый хлеб,
сахари́н и припря́тывает э́то
от всех, выдаёт тёте Да́ше
оди́н раз в день немно́жко
ще́пок на тага́н для гото́вки
обе́да, не позволя́ет сиде́ть
с ла́мпой. (Б. Пильня́к «Три
бра́та» 1923–1928)

Uncle Tolya is a cheapskate,
buying himself white bread and
sugar and hiding it all away,
while giving Aunt Dasha just a
tiny bit of kindling for the trivet
to make dinner, not allowing
her to sit with the lamp.
(Pilnyak, *Three Brothers*,
1923–1928)

Наприме́р, К. всем изве́стная
сте́рва и вы́жига, но по
отноше́нию к Б. спосо́бна
на семе́йный геройзм.
(С. Довла́тов «Арме́йские
пи́сьма к отцу́» 1962–1963)

For example, K. is a well-known
shrew and cheapskate, but when
B. is involved, she is capable
of familial heroism. (Dovlatov,
Army Letters for Father,
1962–1963)

У них лу́чшие в го́роде
оранжере́и, не усту́пят
ца́рским. То́лько садо́вник и
вы́жига же! Дерёт за цветы́
совсе́м не по-бо́жески.
(Н. Ге́йнце «Дочь Вели́кого
Петра́» 1913)

They have the best greenhouses
in the city, no worse than
the imperial ones. Only, the
gardener is such a skinflint!
He bleeds you dry for those
flowers! (Geintse, *The Daughter
of Peter the Great*, 1913)

Выпива́ла

A drunkard. Someone who likes alcohol to an unhealthy extent and
drinks habitually and extensively. Expresses a negative attitude and
scorn.

Conveys the same emotions as its synonyms **поддава́ла**, **пропо́йца**, and
пьянчу́га, and unlike the synonym **выпи́воха**, which conveys fondness, or the neutral **пья́ница**. Used less frequently than other synonyms.

See **выпи́воха**, **поддава́ла**, **пропо́йца**, **пья́ница**, **пьянчу́га**.

Елизаве́та была́ несно́сная
выпива́ла – начина́ла с
са́мого утра.

Elizabeth was an intolerable
drunk – she would begin early in
the morning.

12   *Entries*

Егóр – выпивáла. А рáньше не пил стóлько – э́то началóсь у негó пóсле áрмии.	Yegor didn't used to drink so much – he began after the army.

Выпивóха

A drunkard. Someone who likes alcohol to an unhealthy extent and drinks habitually and extensively. May express fondness and positive feelings, unlike its neutral synonym **пья́ница** and the synonyms **выпивáла**, **поддавáла**, **пропóйца**, and **пьянчýга**, which have nuances at various degree.

See **выпивáла**, **поддавáла**, **пропóйца**, **пья́ница**, **пьянчýга**.

А Абрáмов был егó отéц – тúхий тáйный выпивóха, золоть́е руки, смирнéйший и добрéйший человéк в мúре. (Ю. Домбрóвский «Факультéт ненýжных вещéй» 1978)	Abramov was his father – a quiet, mysterious drunk with magic hands, the gentlest and kindest person in the world. (Dombrovsky, *The Department of Unnecessary Things*, 1978)
Забáвно бы́ло, что учúтель матемáтики, сам большóй выпивóха. (Ф. Искандéр «Гнилáя интеллигéнция и аферúзмы» 2001)	It was amusing that the math teacher was himself a great drunkard. (Iskander, *The Rotten Intelligentsia and Afraudisms,* 2001)
Нúна Петрóвна загáдки не представля́ла – обы́чная ры́хлая добродýшная рýсская бáба, выпивóха, пля́сýнья, балабóлка, существó вполнé безобúдное. (Ю. Нагúбин «Моя́ золотáя тёща» 1994)	Nina Petrovna wasn't a difficult nut to crack – an ordinary, drab, kind-hearted Russian woman, a drunkard, a dancer, a chatterbox – a fairly harmless creature. (Nagibin, *My Golden Mother-in-Law*, 1994)

Вы́скочка

A parvenu. Someone who appears in a society or workplace out of nowhere, having obtained a disproportionately high rank or office, often undeservedly. This person engages in activity that is not necessary and does so to impress someone else. Expresses a strong negative attitude and is very disrespectful.

Entries 13

The same as **нувори́ш** *nouveau-riche* and **парвеню́** *parvenu.* Derived from the verb **вы́скочить** *to jump out.*

The saying **из гря́зи в кня́зи** *from rags to riches* is used about someone who is called **вы́скочка**.

С Ду́мой разгова́ривал не вы́скочка-чино́вник, а госуда́рственный муж. (А. Я́ковлев «О́мут па́мяти» 2001)	It wasn't some parvenu clerk addressing the Duma, but a statesman. (Yakovlev, *The Abyss of Memory*, 2001)
Нача́льница но́вая. Вы́скочка, должно́ быть. Говоря́т, уже ра́зное устро́ила. (Б. Можа́ев «Са́ня» 1957)	She's the new boss. Must be a parvenu. They say she's already given everyone what-for. (Mozhaev, *Sanya*, 1957)
Вы же не сове́тский вы́скочка, как Фоми́н, и вы должны́ понима́ть, что нам бессмы́сленно остава́ться здесь. (М. Шо́лохов «Ти́хий Дон» 1928–1940)	You're not a Soviet parvenu, like Fomin, and you should understand that it's pointless for us to stay here. (Sholokhov, *The Quiet Don*, 1928–1940)
Э́та да́мочка вы́скочка. За душо́й ничего́.	This little lady is a parvenu. She's got an empty soul.

Горемы́ка

A poor soul. A miserable, hopeless person who has experienced misfortune and troubles. Expresses sympathy.

Originates from the noun **го́ре** *sorrow* and the adjective **горемы́чный** *unhappy, doomed.* Synonymous with **бедня́га** and **бедола́га**, but places a greater accent on the misfortune the individual has experienced.

See **бедня́га, бедола́га**.

Одна́ горемы́ка, не суме́в приспосо́биться к наси́льно всу́ченной свобо́де, отрави́лась	One poor soul, unable to get used to the forcefully imposed freedom, poisoned herself with

газом. (О. Но́викова «Же́нский рома́н» 1993)

gas. (Novikova, *A Woman's Novel*, 1993)

Оттараба́нил их наш горемы́ка от звонка́ до звонка́. (А. Росто́вский «По зако́нам во́лчьей ста́и» 2000)

Our poor soul banged them out from bell to bell. (Rostovsky, *According to the Wolf Pack's Laws*, 2000)

Ты б его́ пожале́л. Отпе́тый горемы́ка, поги́бшая душа́. (Б. Пастерна́к «До́ктор Жива́го» 1945–1955)

You'd pity him. A poor wretch whose song was sung, a doomed soul. (Pasternak, *Doctor Zhivago*, 1945–1955)

Грязну́ля

An unwashed and unclean person. Most frequently used when referring to a child. Can express fondness and does not convey a strong negative attitude.

Derived from the noun **грязь** *dirt* and the adjective **гря́зный** *dirty*. The synonymous **замара́шка** also articulates positive feelings, rather than negative ones. Semantically close to **неря́ха**, which expresses disapproval. Antonymous with **чистю́ля**.

See **замара́шка**, **неря́ха**, **чистю́ля**.

Ага́, о́чень гря́зный, большо́й грязну́ля . . . он ведь совсе́м оди́н, дете́й не́ было. (Ю. Три́фонов «Победи́тель» 1960–1970)

Oh yes, a very dirty, large pig . . . he was completely alone, he had no kids. (Trifonov, *The Conqueror*, 1960–1970)

Мой ма́льчик, моя́ грязну́ля, идём в душ.

My boy, my dear little piglet, let's go take a shower.

Я с тобо́й де́ла име́ть не бу́ду, грязну́ля проти́вный. Твоя́ дочь вся в тебя́ – така́я же грязну́ля.

I'm not going to have anything to do with you, you dirty pig. Your little pig daughter takes right after you.

Гулёна

A party animal. Someone who loves to go out, have no responsibilities, and have fun. Can articulate a negative attitude, but more frequently sounds justifying.

Entries 15

Derived from the verb **гуля́ть** *to go out* and the adjective **гуля́щий** *unoccupied*. Semantically close to **гуля́ка**. At the same time, it is used in different contexts and situations.

See **гуля́ка**.

Но как ни ти́хо она́ раздева́лась, Веру́ша просну́лась, се́ла в посте́ли и протяну́ла: Ой, гулёна, гулёна! И где же ты была́ допоздна́? (Г. Никола́ева «Би́тва в пути́» 1959)	But as quietly as she undressed, Verusha woke up, sat up in bed, and drawled out, "Oh, you party animal! And where were you out so late?" (Nikolaeva, *A Battle on the Way*, 1959)
Па́хнет от него́ винцо́м, моро́зом. – Не замёрз, гулёна? – спра́шивает оте́ц. (И. Шмелёв «Ле́то Госпо́дне» 1927–1944)	"He reeks of wine and frost. Not cold, are you, you party animal?" (Shmelev, *God's Summer*, 1927–1944)
Тако́й гулёна – то́лько бы из до́му уйти́. А занима́ться кто бу́дет?	A party animal like him – if only he left home. But then who'll study?
Ну и гулёна же ты, А́нька!	You're such a party animal, An'ka!

Гуля́ка

A party animal, a boozehound. Someone who leads a dissolute and reckless life and enjoys drinking extensively. May imply disapproval, but may also imply the opposite.

Derived from the verb **гуля́ть** *to go out* and the noun **гуля́нка** *party* [inform.]. Semantically close to **гулёна**. However, it can also be used in different contexts and situations. Often combined with such adjectives as **беспе́чный** *carefree*, **бесшаба́шный** *carefree*, and **пра́здный** *unoccupied*.

See **гулёна**.

Останови́лся, погляде́л, как пра́здный гуля́ка, по сторона́м, побрёл не спеша́ всё той же	He stopped, looked around like an indolent boozehound, and then headed towards

набережной к Чернышёву мосту. (Ю. Трифонов «Нетерпение» 1973)

that same riverfront, towards Chernyshev's Bridge. (Trifonov, *Impatience*, 1973)

По нему, посвистывая, прошёл к телефонной будке гуляка, милый и бесхарактерный человек. (В. Аксёнов «Пора, мой друг, пора» 1963)

A boozehound – an amiable fellow, lacking in character – walked right over him on his way to the telephone booth. (Aksenov, *It's Time, My Friend, It's Time*, 1963)

Этот пьяница, курильщик, бабник, обжора, гуляка – мой старший брат. (Б. Ефимов «Десять десятилетий» 2000)

That boozehound, smoker, womanizer, glutton, and drunk is my older brother. (Yefimov, *Ten Decades*, 2000)

Гуляка праздный пьян, хотя и держится привычно бодро, только подсознательно прихрамывая вдруг а-ля Лора. (Э. Лимонов «Молодой негодяй» 1985)

The indolent boozehound is drunk, and though he holds himself in a typically sprightly manner, he is unconsciously limping *à la* Lora. (Limonov, *The Young Rascal*, 1985)

Деляга

Some who only deals with someone or something if there is a profit for him or herself. Conveys strong disapproval and content.

Derived from the noun **дело** *job* and the verb **делать** *to do*. The synonym **делец** *dealmaker* articulates less condemnation than **деляга**.

Ася открылась мне с неожиданной стороны: подхалимка и деляга. (Ю. Нагибин «Дневник» 1983)

I discovered an unexpected side of Asya: sycophantic and self-serving. (Nagibin, *The Diary*, 1983)

Наверное, все здешние: и русские, и тунизийцы, – думают обо мне: «Какая деляга!» (В. Михальский «Одинокому везде пустыня» 2003)

All the locals – Russians and Tunisians – must have thought of me: "What a self-serving bastard!" (Mikhalsky, *Everywhere is a Desert for the Lonely*, 2003)

Entries 17

Учи́тывать э́то никто́ не хоте́л, и ме́ньше всего́ сам заве́дующий пека́рней – широкомо́рдый деля́га, получи́вший срок за каки́е-то спекуляти́вные махина́ции на во́ле. (Г. Жжёнов «Прожито́е» 2002)

Nobody wanted to take this into account, least of all the owner of the bakery – a wide-faced man who only looked out for his own interests and who once got a prison sentence for speculative machinations. (Zhzhonov, *My Life*, 2002)

Я же делово́й челове́к, деля́га, де́лец, как то́лько уню́хаю, что знако́мство мо́жет быть мне вы́годным, тут же на э́ту вы́году набра́сываюсь. (А. Слапо́вский «Ви́сельник» 1994)

I'm a busy man, always keeping an eye out for what can benefit me – as soon as I get a whiff of a relationship being useful to me, I pounce on it immediately. (Slapovsky, *The Hanged Man*, 1994)

Доходя́га

A haggard, half-dead person who evokes sympathy. Frequently used when addressing someone who is close to death. Was used in Stalinist Gulag camps among prisoners.

Derived from the verb **доходи́ть** *to be physically close to death*.

Доходя́га, – доброду́шно улыбну́лся Мохна́ч, кивну́в на измождённого Валька́, сло́вно бы отме́тил в нём заба́вную черту́: про ры́жих таки́м то́ном говоря́т или про щерба́тых. (М. Чула́ки «При́мус» // «Звезда́» 2002)

"He's a goner," smiled Mokhnach in a kindly manner, nodding at the emaciated Valyok, as if noting a fascinating feature about him; people used that sort of tone when noting that someone was a redhead or had a chipped tooth. (Chulaki, "Primus," 2002)

Стару́шка-доходя́га нрав молодо́й сосе́дки не осужда́ла, не замеча́я вокру́г себя́ ничего́, кро́ме ежедне́вной пи́щи. (А. Снегирёв «Ве́ра» 2015)

The moribund old woman did not condemn the neighboring young girl's preferences – she did not notice anything around her other than her daily food. (Snegiryov, *Vera*, 2015)

18 *Entries*

Я вам скажу́, что си́льный мужчи́на куда́ уж скоре́е доплывёт, чем како́й-нибудь доходя́га, скеле́т в бинта́х. (Ю. Домбро́вский «Факульте́т нену́жных веще́й» 1978)	Let me tell you, a strong man is much more likely to make the swim than someone who looks like he should be on his deathbed, a bandaged-up skeleton. (Dombrovsky, *The Department of Unnecessary Things*, 1978)
Посмотри́ на э́ту доходя́гу, совсе́м плоха́.	Just look at that zombie, she looks really bad.

Дури́ла

A fool, an idiot. Used when addressing someone who behaves senselessly and carelessly. Expresses light disapproval.

Semantically close to the noun **дура́к** *fool*.

Да, да, иска́л со́бственную жену́. То́же был молодо́й дури́ла! (В. Мака́нин «Андегра́унд, и́ли геро́й на́шего вре́мени» 1998)	Yes, yes, I was searching for my own wife. I was such a young fool! (Makanin, *Underground, or the Hero of Our Time*, 1998)
Я, зна́чит, туда́-сюда́, ника́к не мог останови́ться, всё иска́л че́стный како́й-нибудь банк, наде́ялся ещё на что-то, дури́ла карто́нная. (А. Грачёв «Я́рый-3. О́рдер на смерть» 2000)	So I was running back and forth, I couldn't stop, I kept searching for an honest bank, I still had hopes, like a fool. (Gratchev, *Furious-3. Death Order*, 2000)
Ну что ты, дури́ла глу́пая, кому́ пове́рила?	You idiot, who did you put your trust in?
Вот дури́ла! Забы́ла, что тебя́ ждут?!	What an idiot! Did you forget that people were waiting for you?

Егоза́

Someone who is restless and full of activity, incapable of sitting still or staying put in one place. Mostly used towards children or young women. Expresses positive feelings.

Entries 19

Semantically close to **непосе́да** and **шалу́н** *unruly child*, **шалу́нья** *unruly child*. Often combined with the noun **юла́** *spinning top* or **стрекоза́** *dragonfly* to emphasize this characteristic.

See **непосе́да**.

Серёжа сиди́, споко́йно, егоза́ ты э́такая, ве́ртишься, как юла́.	Seryozha, sit still, you little fidget, stop squirming like a top.
Это была́ де́вка здоро́вая, смешли́вая, вертля́вая, непосе́да: то ся́дет, то вста́нет, а си́дя повора́чивается к сосе́ду то гру́дью, то спино́й, как егоза́, и непреме́нно заце́пит ло́ктем или коле́ном. (А. Че́хов «Во́ры» 1890)	She was a tall girl, easily amused, restless: she would sit down, then get up, and while sitting, she would turn to her neighbor with her chest, then with her back, inevitably hitting him with an elbow or a knee. (Chekhov, *Thieves*, 1890)
Она́ вела́ себя́, как девчо́нка, как первоку́рсница Ве́ра, баскетболи́стка и егоза́. (В. Аксёнов «Колле́ги» 1962)	She behaved like a little girl, like first grader Vera, like a restless basketball player. (Aksyonov, *Colleagues*, 1962)
Ты и в шестьдеся́т лет . . . бу́дешь така́я же стрекоза́-егоза́. (А. Купри́н «Грана́товый брасле́т» 1911)	You'll be the same restless little dragonfly when you're sixty. (Kuprin, *The Garnet Bracelet*, 1911)

Ехи́дина

A viperish, acid-tongued person who mocks others. Conveys a negative overtone.

Relates to the noun **ехи́дна** *poisonous snake*, the verb **ехи́дничать** *make sarcastic remarks*, and the adjective **ехи́дный** *sarcastic*. **Ехи́дина** sounds stronger than the verb, but weaker than the adjective.

Ага́, попа́лась, ехи́дина! – закрича́л Ми́шка, вскочи́л со скаме́йки и загороди́л ей доро́гу. (А. Дра́бкина «Волше́бные я́блоки» 1975)	"Aha, gotcha, you little viper!" yelled Mishka, jumping up from the bench and blocking her path. (Drabkina, *Magic Apples*, 1975)

Ох, какая ты всё-таки
ехидина, Танюшка, ох-ох,
какая лиса! (В. Аксёнов
«Таинственная страсть» 2007)

Oh, Tanyushka, you're such
a little viper – such a fox!
(Aksyonov, *The Secret Passion*,
2007)

Какой же он ехидина – очень
язвительный и неприятный
человек.

He's such a viper – very snide
and unpleasant.

Идём же к этой ехидине, скажем
ему всё, что думаем о нём.

Let's go to the viper and tell him
everything we think about him.

Жадина (жадюга)

Someone who does not like to share. Is disparaging and disdainful.
Жадюга is stronger and more scornful.

Derived from the adjective **жадный** *greedy*, which sounds less
negative. Semantically close to **сквалыга** and **скряга**, which more
strongly accentuate one's tendency to store and save and express more
negativity. Often used to refer to children. Children themselves use the
phrases **жадина-помадина** and **жадина-говядина** to bully others.

See **сквалыга**, **скряга**.

А Лида добавила нарочно
противным голосом: Жадина-
говядина! Быть жадиной-
говядиной очень стыдно.
(В. Панова «Серёжа» 1955)

And Lida added in an
intentionally unpleasant voice:
Greedy-pants! It was very
shameful being a greedy-pants.
(Panova, *Seryozha*, 1955)

Жабин был из кулачья,
подхалим и жадина.
(С. Довлатов «Армейские
письма к отцу» 1962–1963)

Zhabin was from the kulaks,
a toady, and a greedy bastard.
(Dovlatov, *Army Letters to My
Father*, 1962–1963)

Что-то было такое, когда
я стыдил её и называл
жадиной. [. . .] Считает, что
наказали её справедливо – за
жадность, за то, что булочек
пожалела! (А. Пантелеев
«Наша Маша» 1966)

There was a thing where I
shamed her and called her
greedy. [. . .] She believes that
she was punished justly – for
greed, for the crime of failing to
share her rolls! (Panteleev, *Our
Masha*, 1966)

Эх ты! Жа́дина ты, Пе́тька! Жа́лко мяч? Бои́шься, что не вернём?

Look at you! You're so greedy, Pet'ka! You don't want to give up the ball? You think you won't get it back?

Забия́ка

A bully, a hothead. Someone who is always initiating arguments or fights. Conveys a negative overtone, but might also be condescending. Frequently used by adults as a reproach when addressing children, more often boys, who are trying to start a fight.

Synonymous with **задира**.

See **задира**.

Это солда́тский козёл Филимо́н, знамени́тый на всю у́лицу забия́ка и пья́ница. (К. Чуко́вский «Сере́бряный герб» 1936)

That's the soldiers' goat, Filimon – a well-known rabble-rouser and drunkard. (Chukovsky, *The Silver Emblem*, 1936)

Здоро́вый, как все Рахле́нки, пе́рвый драчу́н и забия́ка на у́лице, но справедли́вый: защища́л сла́бых. (А. Рыбако́в «Тяжёлый песо́к» 1978)

Large, like all Rakhlenkos, first among the bullies and hotheads on the streets, but just: he protected the weak. (Rybakov, *Heavy Sand*, 1978)

В отделе́нии вас и отчита́ют, и отпою́т! – бо́йко отве́тила ему забия́ка-стару́шка. (Е. Звя́гин «Всеми́рная паути́на» // «Звезда́» 2002)

"The police will let you have it, and then they'll sing you a dirge!" responded the trouble-making old woman. (Zvyagin, "The Worldwide Web," 2002)

Весь в отца́ – невероя́тный забия́ка.

He takes right after his father – he's unimaginably hotheaded.

Забулды́га

A drunkard. Someone whose position in life has sunk drastically and who drinks constantly. Typically conveys strong condemnation and is used to refer to males. The diminutive **забулды́жка** expresses more sympathy.

22 *Entries*

The synonymous **пья́ница** and **ханы́га** stress the actual process of drinking, while **забулды́га** places the greater accent on one's social position.

See its synonyms **пья́ница, ханы́га.**

. . . ла́сточка, я́годка неспе́лая, загуби́л её пропо́йный забулды́га, сухопу́тный браконье́р. (В. Аста́фьев «Царь-ры́ба» 1974)

. . . the boozing, drunkard poacher spelled the doom for the little, unripe bird. (Astafyev, *Tsar-Fish*, 1974)

Забулды́га нёс чемода́н, ударя́я то и де́ло себя́ по коле́ну. (С. Довла́тов «Ина́я жизнь» 1984)

The drunkard carried a suitcase that kept smacking into his knee. (Dovlatov, *Another Life*, 1984)

Сосе́дка на́ша – забулды́га стра́шная.

Our neighbor is a terrible drunkard.

Де́ньги все пропила́, дете́й по ми́ру пусти́ла.

She drank through all of her money and set her children loose on the world.

Заводи́ла

Someone who initiates some kind of endeavor. Alternatively, someone who is connoted to be cheerful and who acts as the life of a party or collective, who fires everyone up to do something.

Он был заводи́ла и озорни́к, э́тот семидесятиле́тний пья́ница с то́лстым си́зым но́сом. (Ю. Домбро́вский «Храни́тель дре́вностей» 1964)

He was the life of the party and a prankster, that seventy-year-old drunk with his broad, blue-grey nose. (Dombrovsky, *Keeper of Ancient Things*, 1964)

Не зна́вшим бли́зко Пля́тта тру́дно бы́ло угада́ть в э́том элега́нтном . . . челове́ке отча́янного и до́брого балагу́ра-заводи́лу. (Е. Ве́сник «Дарю́, что по́мню» 1997)

Those who did not know Plyatt well were hard-pressed to see beneath the exterior of this elegant [. . .] man an audacious and kind, rabble-rousing joker. (Vesnik, *I Give What I Remember*, 1997)

Entries 23

Гу́рченко, как мне ка́жется, прекра́сно спра́вилась с ро́лью молодёжной заводи́лы, эдакого темпера́ментного чертёнка в ю́бке. (Э. Ряза́нов «Подведённые ито́ги» 2000)	I felt that Gurchenko was excellent at firing the teens up – she was like a temperamental little imp in a skirt. (Ryazanov, *The Bottom Line*, 2000)
На́шему заводи́ле всё не сиди́тся, уже́ что-то приду́мал.	Our rabble-rouser just can't sit still, he's already come up with something.

Задава́ка (задава́ла)

A showoff. A haughty, self-important, and conceited person. Someone who ostentatiously demonstrates that he/she is the best at something, failing to pay attention to anyone else. Conveys negative feelings.

Derived from the verb **задава́ться** *to have a sense of grandeur about oneself and to show off*. The synonym **зазна́йка** expresses a little less condemnation than **задава́ка**. Semantically close to **вообража́ла**.

See **зазна́йка, вообража́ла**.

Ма́ло того́: он ещё и на «вы» с ней говори́т, Лапши́н, этот злю́ка, этот ненави́стник, этот задава́ка! (С. Солове́йчик «Вата́га «Семь ветро́в» 1979)	Moreover, Lapshin, that spiteful, hateful, showoff uses the formal "you" with her! (Soloveychik, *The "Seven Winds" Band*, 1979)
Ей бы́ли до́роги все, кто свя́зан Ники́той, да́же задава́ка И́нна. (О. Но́викова «Же́нский рома́н» 1993)	Everyone connected to Nikita was dear to her, even that showoff Inna. (Novikova, *A Woman's Novel*, 1993)
Сейча́с ты уви́дишь, како́й я задава́ка! (В. По́стников «Ша́пка-невиди́мка» 1997)	Now you'll see how much of a showoff I am! (Postnikov, *Hat of Invisibility*, 1997)
В кла́ссе И́ра была́ гла́вная задава́ка, и дружи́ли с ней то́лько не́которые девчо́нки.	Ira was the chief showoff in class, and only a few girls were friends with her.

24 *Entries*

Задира

A hothead. The same as **забияка** – someone who provokes arguments or fights. Often refers to children.

Derived from the verb **задираться** *to provoke a fight*.

See **забияка**.

Дéвочка послýшная, уважáемая в грýппе, не задира, дóбрая, а мáльчик тóже óчень хорóший. (В. Шахиджаня́н «1001 вопрóс про ЭТО» 1999)	She was a good girl, respected in the group, not a hothead, kind, and the boy was very good too. (Shakhindzhanian, *1001 Questions About THIS*, 1999)
В тебé задира просыпáется опя́ть. Посиди́ и успокóйся.	The hothead is waking up in you again. Have a seat and calm down.
Знáчит, онá знáла, что Óська ломáка, хвастýн и задира. (Ю. Нагибин «В те ю́ные гóды» 1983)	So she knew that Os'ka was a showoff, a braggart, and a hothead. (Nagibin, *In Those Youthful Years*, 1983)
Почемý хулигáн и задира дя́дя Рóма стал ординáрным чинóвником? (С. Довлáтов «Нáши» 1983)	Why did that hooligan and hothead Uncle Roma become an ordinary government official? (Dovlatov, *Ours*, 1983)

Зазнайка

A smartass. A snobbish and pompous person. Someone who acts as if he/she is the best at something, generally failing to pay attention to anyone else. Conveys a negative overtone.

Derived from the verb **зазнавáться** *to think highly of oneself and to express disdain towards others*. The synonymous **задавáка** articulates a bit more condemnation than **зазнайка**. Semantically close to the nouns **воображáла** and **хвастýн** *braggart*. Antonymous with the adjective **скрóмный** *modest*.

See **задавáка, воображáла**.

Глéбова Антóн привлекáл не тóлько гениáльными спосóбностями, но и тем, что	What was good about Gleb's Anton wasn't just that he was brilliantly talented, but that

	Entries 25
он был скро́мный, не хвасту́н, не зазна́йка. (Ю. Три́фонов «Дом на на́бережной» 1976)	he was modest, that he wasn't a braggart or a smartass. (Trifonov, *The House on the Waterfront*, 1976)
Вдруг ты про́сто зазна́йка, наха́л, и о нас, тебе́ вы́рвавших во́лю, в че́тверть у́ха лишь е́ле слыха́л? (Е. Евтуше́нко «Во́лчий па́спорт» 1999)	What if you're just an insolent smartass and never paid more than half a mind to us, who got you your freedom? (Yevtushenko, *A Wolf's Passport*, 1999)
Вы – дикта́тор, зану́да и высокоме́рный зазна́йка. (Т. Соломати́на «Мой оде́сский язы́к» 2011)	You are a dictator, a buzzkill, and an arrogant smartass. (Solomatina, *My Odessian Tongue*, 2011)
Ишь ты, зазна́йка кака́я! То́лько она́ всё зна́ет и уме́ет.	Look at the smartass! She alone knows everything about everything.

Зайка

Someone who stammers. Although the noun indicates someone's physical deficiency, it can sound offensive, which is why it is better to use the verb **заика́ться**, from which the noun is derived, when addressing someone, as it is stylistically neutral.

The phrase **Так и за́йкой мо́жно/недо́лго стать**, which is used when something sudden and possibly frightening occurs, is commonly used.

Ведь да́же де́тям бы́ло изве́стно, что городско́й прокуро́р е́здит в пода́ренной ему́ плеши́вым за́йкой кладовщико́м «Во́лге». (В. Гро́ссман «Всё течёт» 1955–1963)	Even the kids knew that the local prosecutor drives a Volga that was given to him as a gift by the unkempt, stuttering storekeeper. (Grossman, *Everything Flows*, 1955–1963)
. . . е́сли я затрудня́лся подыска́ть выраже́ние, она́ сама́ помога́ла мне це́лым дождём нетерпели́вых вопро́сов, вро́де тех, кото́рые	. . . if I struggled to find an expression, she herself helped me with a deluge of impatient questions, like those we offer someone with a stutter who gets

26　*Entries*

мы предлага́ем за́йке, мучи́тельно застря́вшему на одно́м сло́ве. (А. Купри́н «Оле́ся» 1896)	agonizingly stuck on a single word. (Kuprin, *Olesya*, 1896)
. . . о́чень прия́тно име́ть э́такого дя́дюшку-за́йку, полко́вника, и всё э́то родство́. (Л. Толсто́й «Ю́ность» 1857)	. . . It's very nice to have an uncle, a colonel, with a stammer like that, and all this family. (Tolstoy, *Youth*, 1857)
Он был за́йкой, но когда́ чита́л ле́кции никогда́ не заика́лся.	He had a stammer, but when he gave lectures, he spoke clearly.

Замара́шка

An unwashed, unclean person. Most frequently used towards children. Can express fondness and does not normally convey a strong negative attitude.

Derived from **замара́ться** *to get dirty*. The synonymous **грязну́ля** also articulates positive feelings, rather than negative ones. Semantically close to **неря́ха**, which expresses disapproval. Associated with the words **Зо́лушка** *Goldilocks*, **принце́сса** *princess*, **принц** *prince*, and such. Antonymous with **чистю́ля**.

See **грязну́ля**, **неря́ха**, **чистю́ля**.

Никто́ не останови́л бе́дную замара́шку и на заста́ве. (Л. Лео́нов «Ру́сский лес» 1950–1953)	Nobody stopped the poor dirty soul at the gatehouse either. (Leonov, *The Russian Woods*, 1950–1953)
Замара́шка Сосо́ не вылеза́л из луж по́дле го́рки цари́цы Тама́ры. (А. Солжени́цын «В кру́ге пе́рвом» 1968)	Dirty little Soso wouldn't get out of the puddles beneath Tsaritsa Tamara's hill. (Solzhenitsyn, *In the First Circle*, 1968)
Моя́ герои́ня вдруг представа́ла преображённой . . . – э́то была́ уже́ не замара́шка с у́лицы, а ле́ди, прекра́сная ле́ди. (Т. Шмы́га «Сча́стье мне улыба́лось. . . » 2000)	My heroine suddenly appeared transformed – she was no longer a slattern from the street, but a lady, a beautiful lady. (Shmyga, *Fortune Smiled on Me*, 2000)

Из ма́ленького замара́шки
он преврати́лся в краси́вого
ста́тного ю́ношу.

The dirty little boy turned into a
handsome, stately youth.

Запева́ла

Someone who starts singing or leads a choir. Figuratively indicates
someone who initiates something.

Ухо́дит ро́та, удаля́ется
от нас навстре́чу судьбе́
ве́чный запева́ла, что́бы
оста́ться в па́мяти молоды́м
и прекра́сным. (В. Реце́птер
«Узло́в, и́ли Обраще́ние к
Казано́ве» 1993)

The squadron is leaving, our
eternal singer is getting farther
away from us to meet destiny,
so that he could stay young and
beautiful. (Recepter, *Uzlov, or
an Address to Casanova*, 1993)

Запева́ла наш запе́л, но то́же
ка́к-то вя́ло, неэнерги́чно,
так что не хоте́лось да́же
подхва́тывать пе́сню.
(В. Солоу́хин «Смех за ле́вым
плечо́м» 1989)

Our singer started singing,
but he wasn't very engaged or
energetic; we didn't even want
to join in. (Soloukhin, *Laughter
Behind the Left Shoulder*, 1989)

По молодо́му го́лосу я
узна́л запева́лу на́шего
самоде́ятельного хо́ра.

I recognized the lead singer of
our amateur choir by the young
voice.

Э́то подполко́вник,
запева́ла и танцо́р, сдви́нув
столы́, образова́л сво́дный
хор всех родо́в войск.
(А. Анфиноге́нов «А внизу́
была́ земля́» 1982)

Having moved the tables to the
sides, the lieutenant-colonel – a
singer and a dancer – created
a mixed choir made up of
different troops. (Anfinogenov,
The World Was Below, 1982)

Зану́да

A tiresome person whose actions elicit annoyance, infuriation, or
boredom. The word might convey disrespect or contempt.

Originates from the verb **нуди́ть** *exhaust* and the adjective **ну́дный**
exhausting.

28　*Entries*

А расска́з зану́ды – э́то
дли́нное изложе́ние того́,
что бы́ло на са́мом де́ле.
(Б. Васи́льев «Огляни́сь на
середи́не» // «Октя́брь», 2003)

A story told by a nudnik is
just a long recitation of facts.
(Vasilyev, "Look Back at the
Middle," 2003)

А э́тот зану́да сказа́л, что ему́
не нра́вятся непунктуа́льные
де́вушки. (М. Тра́уб
«Семёновы» 2009)

That killjoy said that he doesn't
like unpunctual girls. (Traub,
The Semyonovs, 2009)

Я, получа́ется, всю
неде́лю зану́да, пилю́, всё
запреща́ю, придира́юсь,
тре́бую, воспи́-тываю, а ты –
до́бренький, развраща́ешь
ребёнка. (М. Ши́шкин
«Письмо́вник» // «Зна́мя» 2010)

So I'm a hardhat all week long,
I forbid everything, criticize,
demand, and then you come
in and spoil the kid. (Shishkin,
"The Letter Writer," 2010)

Ве́нька, како́й же ты зану́да –
говори́шь, говори́шь.
Переста́нь, надое́ло.

Ven'ka, you're so tedious –
you talk and you talk. Enough
already.

Зева́ка

A bystander. Someone who hangs around without purpose. Used in
combination with the adjectives **пра́здный** *unoccupied*, **у́личный**
street. Conveys disapproval.

Originates from the verb *зева́ть*, which means literally *to yawn* and
figuratively *to be bored* or *to glance around inattentively*. Semantically close to **рази́ня, растя́па**.

See **рази́ня, растя́па**.

. . . но зри́телю я́сно, что э́то
зева́ка, кото́рый ни за что
не пропу́стит интере́сного
зре́лища. (В. Га́ршин
«Заме́тки о худо́жественных
вы́ставках» 1887)

. . . but it is clear to the viewer
that this is an onlooker who
won't miss an interesting
spectacle. (Garshin, *Notes on
Artistic Exhibits*, 1887)

Прохо́дят дни, и я, как зева́ка
на перекрёстке, стою́ и

Days go by, and, like an onlooker
at a crosswalk, I just stand there

Entries 29

любу́юсь. (А. Арбу́зов «Го́ды стра́нствий» 1954)

and feast my eyes. (Arbuzov, *Years of Wandering*, 1954)

Там у него́ стоя́л мольбе́рт, и уже́ собира́лись зева́ки и ребя́та. (Ю. Домбро́вский. «Факульте́т нену́жных веще́й» 1978)

He had an easel next to him, and the onlookers and kids were already gathering. (Dombrovsky, *The Department of Unnecessary Things*, 1978)

На ме́сте ава́рии столпи́лись у́личные зева́ки.

A bunch of bystanders crowded around the scene of the accident.

Злю́ка (злю́чка)

Someone who is constantly enraged; someone who has a bad temper.

Derived from the verb **зли́ться** *to get angry* and the adjective **злой** *angry*. Sometimes associated with the adjective **капри́зный** *whiny*.

И вдруг, ока́зывается, что я . . . ду́маю о тебе́, скве́рной злю́ке. (В. Короле́нко «Пи́сьма» 1889)

And suddenly, it turns out that I'm . . . thinking about you, you hateful shrew. (Korolenko, *Letters*, 1889)

Почему́ капри́зная злю́ка Ане́ля вы́росла са́мой до́брой, че́стной и непритяза́тельной? (С. Довла́тов «На́ши» 1983)

Why did that capricious spitfire Anelya grow up to be kinder, more honest and modest than anyone else? (Dovaltov, *Ours*, 1983)

Гла́вной была́ она́. Таку́ю отврати́тельную злю́ку ре́дко встре́тишь. На лице́, кро́ме раздраже́ния, ничего́. (Л. Гу́рченко «Аплодисме́нты» 1994–2003)

She was most important. Horrid shrews like her are rare. Nothing on her face except for irritation. (Gurchenko, *Applause*, 1994–2003)

Э́тот злю́ка так пло́хо отнёсся к мое́й иде́е, что он встал и смёл всё со стола́!

That man hated my idea so much that he stood up and swept everything off the table!

30   *Entries*

Зубри́ла (зубри́лка)

Someone who is exceptional at rote memorization, but little else. Typically refers to pupils or students and conveys a significant degree of contempt. Can also connote that someone is exemplary, but not necessarily in a positive way.

Derived from the verb **зубри́ть** *memorize by rote* and the noun **зубрёжка** *rote memorization*.

Э́то был чистю́ля, зубри́ла, пе́рвый учени́к, ма́менькин сыно́к. (М. Зо́щенко «Пе́ред восхо́дом со́лнца» 1943)	He was a goody two-shoes, exemplary, best in his class, and a mommy's boy. (Zoshchenko, *Before the Sunrise*, 1943)
А тут я сама́ преврати́лась в зубри́лу, да ещё в морали́стку. (Н. Ильина́ «Доро́ги и су́дьбы» 1957–1985)	And here I myself turned into a stickler for the rules, *and* a moralist. (Ilyina, *Roads and Destinies*, 1957–1985)
Нет, э́тот зубри́ла не люби́л му́зыку, как люби́ла её я . . . (И. Поля́нская «Прохожде́ние те́ни» 1996)	No, that rote memorizer didn't like music as I did . . . (Polyanskaya, *The Passing of the Shadow*, 1996)
В кла́ссе к Зо́е, э́той тихо́не и зубри́ле, относи́лись снисходи́тельно и стара́лись не тро́гать её.	In class, people were condescending towards Zoe, that goody-goody and rote memorizer, and tried to avoid her.

Кале́ка

Someone who is physically disabled, has sustained a serious injury, or who lost a part of his or her body or the ability to control it.

Related to the verb **кале́читься** *to get injured*. **Полторы́ кале́ки** *a cripple and a half* is a humorous, but extremely insensitive expression that is leveled at older, weaker couples.

Обща́ясь с ним, не ве́рилось, что А́лан – кале́ка, с де́тства у него́ но́ги парализо́ваны,	Talking to him, it was difficult to believe that Alan was an invalid, that his legs had been

Entries 31

он хо́дит на костыля́х и так
да́лее. (Д. Гра́нин «Ме́сяц
вверх нога́ми» 1966)

paralyzed since childhood, that
he uses crutches, etc. (Granin,
The Overturned Crescent, 1966)

Она́ вста́ла и обрати́лась
к Джо́нсу с мольбо́й
обрати́ть на неё внима́ние,
помо́чь ей, несча́стной
кале́ке, изуве́ченной бе́лым
води́телем. (Б. Вахти́н «Ги́бель
Джонста́уна» 1978–1980)

She got up and implored Jones
to pay attention to her, to help
her, a poor invalid, handicapped
by a white driver. (Vakhtin,
The Death of Jonestown,
1978–1980)

НЭП был уже́ на исхо́де,
и бы́вшие биржевики́
испу́ганно подава́ли
горла́стому и опа́сному
кале́ке. (Ю. Наги́бин «В те
ю́ные го́ды» 1983)

The NEP was on its way out,
and the frightened former
stockbrokers were serving it
all up to a loud and dangerous
invalid. (Nagibin, *In Those
Youthful Years*, 1983)

Ка́ждое у́тро, проходя́
ми́мо собо́ра, она́ встреча́ла
молодо́го кале́ку.

Every morning, when she
walked by the cathedral, she
saw a young invalid.

Кана́лья

Tends to agree with feminine words, even though it typically refers
to males. Can be used humorously or even to express admiration.
Often combined in phrases with the adjectives **хи́трая** *cunning* and
после́дняя *last*.

Originates from the French *canaille*. Synonymous with **плут** *scoundrel*, **моше́нник** *cheat*, **пройдо́ха**.

See **пройдо́ха**.

Пло́хо у́мер Шами́ль –
как кана́лья бездо́мный.
(В. Гро́мов «Компрома́т для
олига́рха» 2000)

Shamil died poorly, as a
homeless scoundrel.
(Gromov, *Dirt for an Oligarch*,
2000)

Как ты посме́л нару́шить
предписа́ние, кана́лья ты

How dare you violate the
order, you dirty rascal!

32 *Entries*

э́такая! (В. Ко́лышкин «Та́йна
сэ́ра Мо́ррисона» // «Вокру́г
све́та» 1997)

(Kolyshkin, "Sir Morrison's
Secret," 1997)

«Кака́я двусмы́сленная
кана́лья», – ду́мал Самги́н,
наблюда́я Лю́това. (Макси́м
Го́рький «Жизнь Кли́ма
Самгина́» 1928)

"What an equivocating rascal,"
thought Samgin while watching
Lyutov. (Gorky, *The Life of
Klim Samgin*, 1928)

Ну и кана́лья же э́та Ната́лья
Фили́пповна – ни одному́
сло́ву ве́рить нельзя́.

That Natalya Filipovna is such
a sneaky devil – you can't trust
a word she says.

Капризу́ля

A crybaby. Most often a capricious human being or a whimsical
child who cries or is generally stubborn. Can be used tenderly.

The noun originates from the adjective **капри́зный** and the verb
капри́зничать.

Я капризу́ля стра́шная, ты
не ду́май. . . я и нога́ми
то́пать могу́, и крича́ть могу́,
– ты меня́ ещё не зна́ешь
как сле́дует . . . (С. Серге́ев-
Це́нский «Не́дра» 1912)

I'm an awful crybaby, don't
you be getting any ideas. . .
I can stomp my feet and
scream – you don't know me
well enough yet . . . (Sergeev-
Tsensky, *The Depths*, 1912)

Есте́ственно, что бало́ванный,
чуть да́же изне́женный
«недотро́га и капризу́ля» Шу́рка
боя́лся Ко́ли . . . (А. Бенуа́
«Жизнь худо́жника» 1955)

Naturally, the spoiled and
maybe even slightly coddled
prude and crybaby Shurka was
afraid of Kolya . . . (Benoit, *The
Life of an Artist*, 1955)

Уха́живая за капризу́лей
Ма́шенькой, он хорошо́ вы́учил
магази́нную топогра́фию в
райо́не Таври́ческого са́да.
(М. Бако́нина «Де́вять гра́ммов
пласти́та» 2000)

While looking after that
crybaby Mashen'ka, he became
well-acquainted with the layout
of all the stores in the Tavrichesky
Garden area. (Bakonina, *Nine
Grams of Plastic Explosive*, 2000)

Я тебе́ не капризу́ля кака́я-то
– я сама́ всё уме́ю де́лать!

I'm not some crybaby – I know
how to do everything myself!

Entries 33

Книгоно́ша

An archaic word that indicates someone who sells books. In contemporary Russian, it almost exclusively denotes "someone who carries books," but it can on rare occasions be used as a slang term in its archaic meaning.

Originates from the phrase **носи́ть кни́ги** *to carry books*.

Книгоно́шу за́перли в катала́жку, и то́лько ве́чером, стара́ниями Маври́кия Никола́евича, с негодова́нием узна́вшего инти́мные подро́бности э́той га́дкой исто́рии, освободи́ли и вы́проводили из го́рода. (Ф. Достое́вский «Бе́сы» 1871–1872)

They locked the bookseller away in the slammer, and only in the evening did the efforts of Mauriky Nikolaevich, who discovered the intimate details of the sordid tale, lead to his being released and escorted out of town. (Dostoevsky, *Demons*, 1871–1872)

«Я – книгоно́ша», – говори́ла она́, вынима́я из су́мки то стихи́ Корни́лова, то́лько что напеча́танные в «Но́вом ми́ре», то по́весть Ги́нзбург, ещё не напеча́танную нигде́. (Л. Чуко́вская «Па́мяти Фри́ды» 1966–1967)

"I am a bookseller," she would say, taking out of her purse Kornilov poems, freshly published in *Novy Mir*, or a Ginzburg short story that hadn't been published anywhere yet. (Chukovskaya, *Memories About Frida*, 1966–1967)

Книгоно́ша получа́ет ми́зерное жа́лованье, но име́ет пра́во на определённые проце́нты с прода́жи книг. (Э. Лимо́нов «Молодо́й негодя́й» 1985)

A bookseller gets a meager wage, but can pocket some percentage from every book sold. (Limonov, *The Young Villain*, 1985)

По́сле войны́ жил в Сара́тове и Росто́ве-на-Дону́, рабо́тал воспита́телем в детдо́ме, рабо́чим сце́ны, в Москве́ – киоскёром и книгоно́шей; восстано́влен в

After the war, he lived in Saratov and Rostov-on-Don, worked as a schoolteacher and a stageworker, then in Moscow as a kiosk owner and bookseller; he is reinstated as a Party

34 *Entries*

па́ртии и в Сою́зе писа́телей. (А. Иличе́вский «Перс» 2009)	member and a member of the Writers' Guild. (Ilichevsky, *The Persian*, 2009)

Колле́га

A colleague. Used by someone who works in an intellectual field to refer to a coworker. Occasionally, people also use it when addressing someone of the same profession or area of expertise. Tends to refer to males.

Synonymous with **сотру́дник** *coworker*.

Как-то меня́ допра́шивал мой колле́га, мы одного́ с ним вы́пуска . . . (Ю. Домбро́вский. «Факульте́т ненужных веще́й» 1978)	My colleague once subjected me to an interrogation – he and I were classmates . . . (Dombrovsky, *The Department of Unnecessary Things*, 1978)
Я всё де́лала сама́, а мой ста́рший колле́га ни во что не вме́шивался . . . (И. Архи́пова «Му́зыка жи́зни» 1996)	I did everything myself, while my senior colleague stayed out of it all. (Arkhipova, *The Music of Life*, 1996)
Не она́ – Екатери́на Миха́йловна. Кото́рая уда́рила Ли́дию Тимофе́евну по лицу́. Свою́ молоду́ю колле́гу. (А. Гела́симов «Фокс Ма́лдер похо́ж на свинью́» 2001)	She's not the one – it was Ekaterina Mikhailovna. The one who hit Lidia Timofeevna in her face. Her young colleague. (Gelasimov, *Fox Malder Looks Like a Pig*, 2001)
Мы как бы вы́несем на́шего колле́гу за ско́бки. (С. Но́сов «Фигу́рные ско́бки» 2015)	We will, shall we say, turn a blind eye on our colleague. (Nosov, *Figure Parentheses*, 2015)

Копу́ша

A slowpoke. Typically used to refer to children who do things slowly. Does not convey a negative attitude and can actually express fondness.

Originates from the verb **копа́ться** *to do something very slowly*.

Entries 35

Éсли ты за́втра не пу́стишь маши́ну, я тебя́ в мо́ре без корабля́ пущу́, копу́ша, чёрт! (А. Плато́нов «Сокрове́нный челове́к» 1928)

If you don't turn on the machine tomorrow, I'll set you afloat without a boat, you sluggard, damn it! (Platonov, *The Secret Person*, 1928)

Иногда́, éсли она́ и заво́зится в огоро́де и́ли с детьми́ . . . Ну да, копу́ша она́ у меня́ . . . (Ф. Исканде́р «Сандро́ из Чеге́ма» 1989)

Sometimes, even if she does linger in the garden . . . Well, yeah, she's my little slowpoke . . . (Iskander, *Sandro From Chegem,* 1989)

Меня́ всегда́ торопи́ли ребя́та из на́шего кла́сса и физру́к: «Поскоре́е, что ты так до́лго мо́ешься, копу́ша, пойдём, тебя́ все ждут». (В. Шахиджаня́н «1001 вопро́с про ЭТО» 1999)

My classmates and coach would always rush me: "Faster, slowpoke, what are you doing in the shower so long, let's go, everyone's waiting for you." (Shakhidzhanyan, *1001 Questions About THAT*, 1999)

Ничего́ не мо́жем сде́лать с Таню́шкой – копу́ша ужа́сная, ничего́ не успева́ет.

We don't know what to do about Tanyushka – she's a horrible slowpoke, she can't manage to finish anything.

Коротышка

"Shorty" or "munchkin". Someone who is short. Generally stylistically neutral, though it can convey a negative overtone. Stereotypically refers to males and indicates a stout, short man.

Originates from the adjective **коро́ткий** *short*. The synonymous **коротыш** *shorty* is used less frequently.

Сиди́ уж, – и поспеши́ла сле́дом за коротышкой в другу́ю ко́мнату. (В. Аста́фьев «Послéдний поклóн» 1968–1991)

"Just sit," she said and rushed after the short man into the other room. (Astafyev, *The Last Bow*, 1968–1991)

Он входи́л в Кра́сную столо́вую, чуть пригну́вшись

The shorty, his hat adding half his height again, would come

в дверя́х, – короты́шка, метр
с ке́пкой, и остана́вливался
в вели́чественной по́зе.
(Ю. Бу́йда «Расска́зы о
любви́» // «Но́вый Мир» 1999)

into the Red dining room,
bending a little in the door, and
would stand there in a majestic
pose. (Buida, "Tales about
Love," 1999)

Но́вого команди́ра на о́бщем
построе́нии ли́чного соста́ва
полка́ предста́вил собра́вшимся
толстя́к-короты́шка в ши́том
золото́м адмира́льском
мунди́ре, с ко́ртиком на
бедре́. (В. Сини́цына «Му́за и
генера́л» 2002)

When the regiment was in
formation, a short and stout
man in a gold-embroidered
admiral's uniform with a dagger
at his side introduced the new
commander. (Sinitsyna, *The
Muse and the General*, 2002)

Э́то Ди́мыч с лопа́той, –
говори́л пу́хлый короты́шка,
ты́кая па́льцем в фотогра́фию.
(А. Сапе́гина «Ещё раз о Бу́нине» //
«Сиби́рские огни́» 2012)

"That's Dimych with the shovel
there," said the munchkin,
pointing at the photograph.
(Sapegina, "One More Time
About Bunin," 2012)

Кривля́ка

Someone who makes faces or imitates others to show off. Conveys
disapproval and disdain.

Derived from the verb **кривля́ться** *to make faces*. Semantically
close to **лома́ка**, a noun that indicates someone who uses his body
to show off, as opposed to just his face.

See **лома́ка**.

Она́ кривля́ка, она́ вся
иску́сственна. Кто не зна́ет
её? (С. Волко́нский «Мои́
воспомина́ния» 1923–1924)

She puts on airs, she's
completely fake. Who doesn't
know her? (Volkonsky, *My
Memories*, 1923–1924)

Кака́я-то Ми́ртова, поэте́сса,
ка́жется, из Ки́ева, кривля́ка,
гро́мче всех говори́ла и
ба́сом хохота́ла не к ме́сту.
(М. Ши́шкин «Вене́рин
во́лос» // «Зна́мя» 2005)

One Mirtova, a poetess from Kiev,
I think, likes to make faces – she
talked louder than everyone, and
her low laughter could be heard
rumbling in all the wrong places.
(Shishkin, "Venus's Hair," 2005)

Опя́ть яви́лся со свое́й
жено́й-кривля́кой – всё вре́мя
каки́е-то ро́жи ко́рчит.

He came with his mugger of a
wife again – she's constantly
making faces.

Пе́тька кривля́ка, ведёт себя́,
как шут горо́ховый.

Pet'ka is an ape, he behaves
like a buffoon.

Кровопи́йца

A bloodsucker. A cruel, ruthless, and pitiless person. Strongly conveys a negative attitude towards the referenced individual person. At the same time, the noun can exaggerate statements and be used with a degree of humor.

This is a compound noun made up of the noun **кровь** *blood* and the verb **пить** *to drink*.

И в да́нном слу́чае вы ви́дите
её [и́стину] в том, что я
кровопи́йца и послужи́ла
причи́ной ги́бели двух
люби́мых мно́ю люде́й?
(А. Ким «Бе́лка» 1984)

And in the situation at hand,
do you see the truth that I'm
a bloodsucker who caused the
deaths of two people I loved?
(Kim, *The Squirrel*, 1984)

Ба́бушка объясни́ла
мне, что дя́дя То́ля –
ка́рлик-кровопи́йца, кото́рый
хо́чет перее́хать в Москву́ и
всё у нас отобра́ть. (П. Сана́ев
«Похорони́те меня́ за
пли́нтусом» 1996)

Grandma explained to me that
Uncle Tolya is a bloodsucking
little dwarf who wants to move
to Moscow and take everything
away from us. (Sanaev, *Bury
Me Behind the Baseboard*,
1996)

Мини́стров встреча́ли
враждébно, ча́сто раздава́лись
оскорби́тельные вы́крики:
«Пала́ч!», «Кровопи́йца!»
(Г. Иоффе «О́бщество
бы́ло утомлено́. Исто́рия
«Вы́боргского воззва́ния» //
«Нау́ка и жизнь» 2006)

The ministers received a
hostile welcome, with cries of:
"Executioner! Bloodsucker!"
(Ioffe, "Society Was Tired.
A History of the Vyborg
Manifesto," 2006)

Наро́д в го́роде называ́л мэ́ра
тира́ном и кровопи́йцей.

The townspeople called the
mayor a tyrant and a bloodsucker.

38   *Entries*

Кро́ха

A little child. Can also indicate a small person. Expresses fondness.

The nouns **крохоту́ля** and **крохоту́лечка** denote a greater degree of smallness, and they are derived from **кро́ха**; the latter is derived from the adjective **кро́хотный** *tiny*. The nouns **кро́шка**, **малы́ш** *little one*, and **малы́шка** *little one* are synonyms. Semantically close to **коро́тышка**.

See **коро́тышка**, **кро́шка**.

Да́же е́сли ва́шему кро́хе не́сколько неде́ль, всё равно́ вы для него́ воплоще́ние си́лы и могу́щества. (Р. Казако́в «Отцо́вский инсти́нкт» // «Семе́йный до́ктор» 2002)	Even if your baby boy is just a few weeks old, he still already sees you as the manifestation of strength and might. (Kazakov, "Paternal Instinct," 2002)
Совсе́м ма́ленький ма́льчик, су́щая кро́ха, одни́ ко́сточки, коле́ночки торча́т, – сиди́т и го́рько-го́рько пла́чет. (А. Щёголев «Чёрная сторона́ зе́ркала» 2014)	A very small boy, a veritable baby, nothing but bones, his knees sticking out – he's sitting and crying bitterly. (Shchyogolev, *The Dark Side of the Mirror*, 2014)
А́ллочка, така́я кро́ха, ещё не говори́т, а уже́ танцу́ет и му́зыку чу́вствует.	Allochka is still such a baby; she doesn't even speak yet, but already dances and feels musical rhythms.
Кто же его́ тако́го кро́ху бро́сит одного́?	Who would ever leave a little tyke like him all alone?

Кро́шка

A little child. Also indicates a small person, typically a young woman. Expresses fondness.

The nouns **кро́ха**, **малы́ш** *little one*, and **малы́шка** *little one* are synonyms. Semantically close to **коро́тышка**.

See **коро́тышка**, **кро́ха**.

Он кре́пнет, э́тот кро́шка-были́нка, и я ве́рю, зна́ю, что насту́пит и в мое́й жи́зни лу́чшее вре́мя. (А. Колмого́ров «Мне доста́вшееся: Семе́йные хро́ники Наде́жды Лухма́новой» 2012)

That tiny little thing is getting stronger, and I believe, I know that better times will come in my life too. (Kolmogorov, *What I Got: The Family Chronicles of Nadezdha Lukhmanova*, 2012)

Не пове́рите: кро́шкой был, три го́дика, но почему́-то запечатле́лась в па́мяти э́та сце́на. (Д. Ру́бина «Ме́дная шкату́лка» 2015)

You won't believe it: I was still a baby, only three years old, but for some reason, that scene stayed in my memory. (Rubina, *The Copper Box*, 2015)

Их мла́дшему кро́шке исполнилось два года.

Their littlest one just turned two.

Кро́шку, ма́ленькую краса́вицу, зову́т Ни́на.

That pretty little thing is called Nina.

Кути́ла

A debauchee. Someone who revels, celebrates wildly, leads a reckless life, and generally spends a lot of money. Typically refers to males. The noun does not convey strong negative emotions and can even express positive feelings.

Derived from the verb **кути́ть** *carouse* and the noun **кутёж** *bender*. The expression **прожига́тель жи́зни** *wastrel* is a synonym, as well as **про́жига,** which evokes stronger negative overtone. Semantically close to **гуля́ка** and **пове́са**.

See **гуля́ка**, **про́жига**.

И не то чтоб все они́ бы́ли кути́лы, ины́е, напро́тив, прекра́сные мужья́ и отцы́, но де́ньги мо́жно мота́ть и кути́ле и прекра́сному отцу́. (Ф. Достое́вский «Дневни́к писа́теля» 1877)

And it's not that they were all debauchees; on the contrary, they were wonderful husbands and fathers, but a wastrel and a wonderful father are both capable of blazing through money. (Dostoevsky, *A Writer's Diary*, 1877)

Это его прия́тель, – поясни́ла
Мари́я, – большо́й кути́ла и
о́чень до́брый челове́к, совсе́м
родно́й . . . (Б. Окуджа́ва
«Путеше́ствие дилета́нтов»
1971–1977)

"His buddy's the debauchee
and very kind, dear man,"
explained Maria. (Okudzhava,
The Dilettantes' Adventure,
1971–1977)

Оди́н Михаи́л Толсто́й . . .
был типи́чным прожига́телем
жи́зни, кути́лой, гитари́стом,
исполни́телем цыга́нских
рома́нсов. (С. Голи́цын
«Запи́ски уцеле́вшего.
Предисло́вие» 1989)

Only Mikhail Tolstoy . . . was
a typical bon vivant, wastrel
guitarist, a player of Gypsy
songs. (Golitsyn, *Notes of a
Survivor. Preface*, 1989)

Она́ вы́шла за́муж за
легкомы́сленного челове́ка,
кути́лу и ужа́сного игрока́.

She married a frivolous man – a
debauchee and a gambler.

Ла́комка

Someone who enjoys tasty and sweet food.

Derived from the adjective **ла́комый** *dainty* and the noun
ла́комство *delicacy*. Semantically close to the nouns **сласте́на** and
сладкое́жка.

See **сладкое́жка**, **сласте́на**.

Он диви́лся и уверя́л, что
то́лько така́я ла́комка, как
я, могла́ разыска́ть столь
вку́сные ве́щи. (А. Достое́вская
«Воспомина́ния» 1911–1916)

He looked on and asserted that
only a gourmand like me could
find such delicious things.
(Dostoevskaya, *Memoirs*,
1911–1916)

. . . он по́тчевал меня́
пря́никами, до кото́рых я был
большо́й ла́комка . . . (А. Бенуа́
«Жизнь худо́жника» 1955)

. . . he treated me with
gingerbread, for which I had a
serious sweet tooth. (Benoit, *An
Artist's Life*, 1955)

Ю́ра не ужа́сный ла́комка, но
иногда́ оди́н съеда́л це́лую

Yura doesn't have the biggest
sweet tooth, but he would

Entries 41

бáнку вишнёвого варéнья.	sometimes eat an entire jar of cherry preserves by himself.
Тóлько такóй лáкомка, как ты, мóжет нóчью плóтно есть.	Only another gourmand like you could eat so much at night.

Лáпушка

An affectionate address to a person, predominantly to women and children.

Usually feminine pronouns are combined with it regardless of the biological gender of the referred person: **моя́ лáпушка** *sweetie*.

Лáпушка моя́, Григóрий Пантелéвич! Перевоевáть нáдо! (М. Шóлохов «Тíхий Дон» 1928–1940)	My dear Grigory Pantelevich! We have to refight it! (Sholokhov, *The Quiet Don*, 1928–1940)
Спи, дúтятко, Спи, лáпушка, Спи, мáленький, Спи, сóлнышко . . . (Ю. Гéрман «Россúя молодáя» 1952)	Sleep, child, sleep, dearie, sleep little one, sleep, sunshine . . . (German, *Young Russia*, 1952)
А éсли вспóмнить тот кошмáр, котóрый емý навязáла мáтушка в сентябрé, так э́та по сравнéнию с той прóсто лáпушка. (М. Зосúмкина «Ты проснёшься» 2015)	And if you recall the horror that his mother hooked him up with back in September, then by comparison, this one is just a dear. (Zosimkina, *You Will Wake Up*, 2015)

Лгунúшка

A diminutive form of **лгун** *liar*. While the latter conveys a negative attitude, **лгунúшка** can express fondness when addressing children, despite implying disapproval. Typically used to refer to children and males.

The synonymous **лжец** *liar* and **врун** *liar* have a strong negative overtone, while **врунúшка** expresses the same emotion as **лгунúшка**. Often used with the adjective **жáлкий** *pitiful*.

See **врунúшка**, **хвастунúшка**.

42   *Entries*

Вы, господа́, пожа́луйста, не ве́рьте ни в чём Ха́рикову: он ужа́сный лгуни́шка и непреме́нно вам на меня́ что́-нибудь налжёт. (А. Пи́семский «Ру́сские лгуны́» 1865)

Gentlemen, please, do not take Harikov at his word on anything: he's a terrible liar, and he'll inevitably tell you a lie about me. (Pisemsky, *Russian Liars*, 1865)

Он жа́лкий лгуни́шка, хвасту́н, устро́ился в тылу́ и врёт всем, что изобрета́ет что́-то. (А. Арбу́зов «Го́ды стра́нствий» 1954)

He's a dirty liar and a braggart; he trails behind everyone and keeps telling everyone that he's inventing something. (Arbuzov, *Years of Travel*, 1954)

В кла́ссе все смея́лись над хвастли́вым лгуни́шкой, кото́рый всегда́ что́-нибудь да выду́мывал.

Everyone in class laughed at the boastful little liar who always came up with some story or other.

Никто́ не ве́рил Ка́те, изве́стной лгуни́шке, да́же когда́ она́ говори́ла пра́вду.

Nobody ever believed Katya, a well-known liar, even when she told the truth.

Лежебо́ка

A lazybones. Someone who likes to sleep or just lie around. Conveys a negative overtone.

Can be synonymous with **безде́льник** *idler*, **лентя́й** *lazybones*, **ло́дырь** *idler*. Semantically close to **лентяю́га**. Can be combined with the adjective **беспе́чный** *careless*.

See **лентяю́га**.

. . . из ре́звой и весёлой хохоту́шки преврати́лась в мра́чную лежебо́ку, стра́стную кури́тельницу дороги́х благово́нных папиро́с и усе́рдную поглоти́тельницу души́стых ликёров. (А. Амфитеа́тров «Ма́рья Лу́сьева» 1903)

. . . She turned from a frisky and vibrant woman into a somber lazybones, a passionate enthusiast of expensive, aromatic cigarettes, and an assiduous imbiber of heady liqueurs. (Amfiteatrov, *Maria Lusyeva*, 1903)

Беспе́чный лежебо́ка и
пьянчу́жка очути́лся ни с
того́ ни с сего́ в положе́нии
челове́ка за́нятого,
озабо́ченного, спеша́щего
и да́же бо́рющегося с
приро́дой. (А. Че́хов «Го́ре»
1885–1886)

The careless sluggard and
drunkard found himself all
of a sudden in the position of
someone busy, preoccupied,
harried, and even fighting
against nature. (Chekhov,
Sorrow, 1885–1886)

Ну что ты всё валя́ешься,
лежебо́ка ты э́такая, встава́й
тебе́ говоря́т.

Why are you still lying around,
you lazybones, I said get up?

У тебя́, лени́вого лежебо́ки,
всё в до́ме разва́ливается, а
ты и в ус не ду́ешь.

Your house is falling apart, you
bum, and you don't even give
a damn.

Лентяю́га

A lazy person. Does not convey a strong negative overtone and can
often be used fondly to refer to children.

The noun **лентя́й** *lazybones*, from which **лентяю́га** is derived, and
the synonymous **безде́льник** *idler* express stronger negativity than
лентяю́га. Semantically close to **лежебо́ка**.

See **лежебо́ка**.

Ну́жно э́того лентяю́гу в а́рмию
отда́ть, ина́че так и пролежи́т
на дива́не всю жизнь.

That lazy bum should be sent to
the army, or else he'll spend his
whole life on that couch.

Посмотри́те на э́ту лентяю́гу!
Ты опя́ть валя́ешься? Встань
и займи́сь де́лом.

Look at this lazy bum! You're
lying around again? Get up and
do some work.

Твой брат бессо́вестный
лентяю́га – никогда́ ниче́м не
помо́жет.

Your brother is a shameless
bum – he never helps out with
anything.

Уво́лили её за то, что бе́здарь
и ужа́сная лентяю́га.

She was fired for mediocre
performance and for being a
lazy bum.

44   *Entries*

Ловчи́ла

A crafty, cunning individual. Strongly negative and disrespectful.

Derived from the verb **ловчи́ть** *to be crafty/to play with loaded dice* and the adjective **ло́вкий** *deft.* Associated with adjectives like **изворо́тливый** *elusive*, **хи́трый** *cunning* and the noun **моше́нник** *swindler*. Synonymous with **проны́ра**.

See **проны́ра**.

Его́ принима́ли за ловчи́лу, о́чень изобрета́тельного, кото́рый успе́шно и стреми́тельно де́лал карье́ру. (Ю. Три́фонов «Дом на на́бережной» 1976)	He was seen as a very artful trickster who was successfully and determinedly climbing up the career ladder. (Trifonov, *The House on the Waterfront*, 1976)
Оказа́лось, что . . . он де́лает «ле́вые» за́писи популя́рных певцо́в и и́ми торгу́ет – в о́бщем, деле́ц и ловчи́ла. (Д. Карапетя́н «Влади́мир Высо́цкий. Воспомина́ния» 2000–2002)	It turned out . . . that he makes illegal recordings of popular singers and sells them; put plainly, he was a hustler. (Karapetyan, *Vladimir Vysotsky: Recollections*, 2000–2002)
И́горь уже́ давно́ не был ловчи́лой, занима́вшимся фарцо́й, а стал соли́дным бизнесме́ном.	Igor wasn't a hustler involved with the black market anymore and had long since become a respected businessman.
Дире́ктор магази́на – изве́стная ловчи́ла и спекуля́нтка.	The store manager was a well-known hustler and profiteer.

Лома́ка

A showoff. Someone who likes to show off. Conveys disapproval and disdain.

Derived from the verb **лома́ться** *to show off*. Semantically close to **кривля́ка**, a noun that indicates someone who uses his face to show off, as opposed to his whole body.

See **кривля́ка**.

Конéчно, Дёмин – ломáка,
лю́бит попозúровать, но что
он глуп, э́того никтó не скáжет.
(И. Э́ренбург «Óттепель» 1954)

Of course Dyomin is a showoff,
he loves to pose, but nobody
can call him a fool. (Ehrenburg,
The Thaw, 1954)

Онá немнóго ломáка. Онá
чем-то недовóльна собóй,
ей что-то в себé самóй не
нрáвится. (Б. Пастернáк
«Дóктор Живáго» 1957)

She's a bit of a showoff. She's
not quite pleased with herself,
she doesn't like something
about herself. (Pasternak,
Doctor Zhivago, 1957)

Антóн невыносúмый ломáка –
хóдит, задрáв гóлову, и стрóит
из себя́ велúкого худóжника.

Anton is an unbearable showoff –
he walks around, nose in the air,
acting like he's a great artist.

Зóя былá не похóжа на свою́
сестру́ – ломáку и воображáлу.

Zoya was nothing like her sister –
a showoff and a poser.

Мазúла[1]

Figuratively an inept artist. Conveys contempt, disdain.

Derives from the verb **мáзать** *to spread something on a surface.*

. . . из худóжника он
превратúлся в полуголóдного
мазúлу и зарабáтывал на
хлеб рисовáнием лóзунгов
и плакáтов. (Ю. Трúфонов
«Другáя жизнь» 1975)

. . . he turned from an artist into
a half-starving doodler and put
bread on the table by drawing
slogans and posters. (Trifonov,
Another Life, 1975)

Бездáрные мазúлы! Я вúдел
там, – он махну́л рукóй в
стóрону дóма, – вáшу мазню́.
(И. Стрелкóва «Похищéние
из провинциáльного музéя»
1980)

"Mediocre doodlers! I've
seen your doodles," he said,
waving in the direction of the
house. (Strelkova, *A Heist in a
Provincial Museum*, 1980)

Мазúла, как заглáзно егó
называ́ли, понимáл, в
отлúчие от мнóгих, так егó
называ́ющих, свой ску́дные
возмóжности, а тем пáче

The doodler, as people
called him behind his back,
understood, unlike many who
called him that, his meager
abilities and especially his

познáния в йконописи.
(И. Лиснянская «Величинá
и фýнкция» // «Знáмя» 1999)

knowledge of icon painting.
(Lisnyanskaya, "Greatness
and Function," 1999)

Дýмаю, и на том свéте
я обреченá позúровать
какóму-нибудь тáмошнему
мазúле. (Д. Рýбина «Мéдная
шкатýлка» 2015)

I think that even in my next life,
I'm doomed to pose for some
celestial doodler. (Rubina, *The
Copper Box*, 2015)

Мазúла[2]

In sports, someone who misses their mark, particularly in shooting or soccer. Conveys disdain and disrespect, but occasionally is merely condescending.

Derived from the verb **мáзать** *to miss*. Often used with the adjective **бездáрный** *mediocre*.

Большинствó игрáть не
умéло. Профессóру кричáли:
«Мазúла!» Он виновáто
улыбáлся и бéгал за мячóм
в колючий кустáрник.
(С. Антóнов «Разноцвéтные
кáмешки» // «Огонёк» 1959)

The majority did not know
how to play. "You missed!"
They yelled at the professor.
He would smile sheepishly
and race after the ball into
the thorny shrubs. (Antonov,
"Multicolored Pebbles," 1959)

. . . крóшечный Пелé . . .
демонстрúровал филигрáнную
тéхнику и всё врéмя выводúл
на удáр своегó партнёра –
бездáрного мазúлу. . .
(Ю. Нагúбин «Дневнúк» 1969)

. . . the tiny Pele demonstrated
flawless technique and
constantly set his talentless
partner up for a clean shot.
(Nagibin, *The Diary*, 1969)

«Бей! Пасýй! Мазúла! Гол!»
От э́того шýма в тúхой
кóмнате ещё спокóйнее.
(Л. Матвéева «Продлёнка»
1987)

"Take it! Pass! He misses!
Goal!" All the noise made
the quiet room even calmer.
(Matveeva, *Afterschool*, 1987)

Я вы́стрелил и. . . промáзал.
«Эх ты, мазúла», – вéсело

I shot and . . . missed. "What a
sharpshooter," said Ovechkin

Entries 47

сказа́л Ове́чкин. (В. Молча́нов «Дороги́е страни́цы па́мяти» // «Наш совреме́нник» 2004)

merrily. (Molchanov, "The Dear Pages of Memory," 2004)

Малю́тка

A short person or someone young. Typically refers to children. Conveys tenderness.

Derived from the adjective **ма́ленький** *small*. Semantically close to the noun **маля́вка**, which can be used disdainfully.

See **маля́вка**.

Де́вушка оказа́лась о́чень ю́ной, почти́ малю́ткой, с туги́м ли́чиком. (Н. Саду́р «Не́мец» 1996)

The girl turned out to be very young, almost a toddler, with a taught face. (Sadur, *The German*, 1996)

У него́ когда́-то давно́ умерла́ молода́я жена́, оста́лся сын-малю́тка. (Д. Ру́бина «Ру́сская канаре́йка. Блу́дный сын» 2014)

His young wife died a long time ago, leaving a little boy. (Rubina, *The Russian Canary. The Prodigal Son*, 2014)

Э́той малю́тке всего́ двена́дцать лет.

That little thing is only twelve.

Пришли́ на́ши друзья́ с двумя́ сыновья́ми – десятиле́тним Воло́дей и малю́ткой Се́нечкой.

Our friends came over with their two sons – ten-year-old Volodya and tiny little Senechka.

Маля́вка

Indicates someone who is smaller or younger when compared with someone else. Typically used to refer to children. Can sound patronizing or fond, depending on the situation.

Derives from the adjective **ма́ленький** *small*. Semantically close to **малю́тка**, which cannot be used disdainfully.

See **малю́тка**.

48   *Entries*

. . . по́сле выпускно́го ве́чера они́ всем кла́ссом отпра́вились на парохо́де до Го́рького, и вме́сте с ма́терью-буфе́тчицей была́ в той пое́здке Си́ма, маля́вка-восьмикла́ссница. (А. Анфиноге́нов «А внизу́ была́ земля́» 1982)

. . . after graduation, the whole class took a ship to Gorky, and Sima, a wee eighth grader, was there, together with her mother, a barmaid. (Anfinogenov, *The Earth Was Below*, 1982)

. . . в э́ту мину́ту кто-то невзра́чный, маля́вка из мла́дшего кла́сса, подошёл к нему́ и веле́л идти́ туда́. (Б. Хаза́нов «Похо́ж на челове́ка» 1999)

. . . at that moment, some insignificant kid, a wee thing from a lower grade, came up to him and ordered him to leave. (Khazanov, *He Looks Like a Person*, 1999)

Тебя́ бы я, коне́чно, не узна́л. Ты ж совсе́м была́ маля́вка. А вот Зи́нку я сра́зу узна́л! (Г. Щербако́ва «Ах, Ма́ня. . .» 2002)

I wouldn't have recognized you, of course. You were a wee little thing. But Zinka I recognized right away! (Shcherbakova, *Oh, Manya . . .* 2002)

Собира́лись все взро́слые, и на него́, маля́вку, никто́ внима́ния не обраща́л.

It was a gathering of adults, and nobody paid attention to him, the little tyke.

Миля́га

Refers to someone nice. Typically addresses males. Evokes positive feelings, such as fondness, but can be scornful and disparaging. Informal and expresses familiarity.

Derived from the adjective **ми́лый** *sweet*. The synonymous **ми́лый челове́к** *dear person* is more neutral. Synonymous with **симпатя́га**. The phrase **миля́га-па́рень** *nice young man* is commonly used in discourse when referring to a male.

See **симпатя́га**.

«Ох, уж э́тот Ни́конов», – поду́мал он, – «миля́га па́рень, но звёзд с не́ба не хвата́ет». (М. Алда́нов «Ключ» 1929)

"Oh, that Nikonov," he thought. "A dear young man, but he really isn't too bright." (Aldanov, *The Key*, 1929)

Entries   49

Коне́чно, тво́я стару́ха Ашхе́н – миля́га! Но она́ же стару́ха! (Ю. Ге́рман «Дорого́й мой челове́к» 1961)

Your old woman, Ashkhen, is a dear person! But she's still an old woman! (German, *My Dear Man*, 1961)

Софро́нов, хлебосо́льный, раду́шный хозя́ин, провозглаша́л то́сты, шути́л, чита́л стихи́, пел под гита́ру – миля́га па́рень, свой в до́ску, ду́шка, да и то́лько! (М. Козако́в «Актёрская кни́га» 1978–1995)

Sofronov, a hospitable, kindhearted man, said toasts, joked, read poetry, sang with a guitar – a dear man, one of our own, a kindred spirit! (Kozakov, *The Actor's Book*, 1978–1995)

Молодчи́на (молодча́га)

An informal expression of praise. **Молодча́га** is even more stylistically informal than **молодчи́на** and is used less frequently.

The synonymous **молоде́ц** (a word used to convey the meaning of "good job") and **у́мница** are more formal.

See **у́мница**.

И он, молодчи́на, тре́бует освобожде́ния поли́т-зэ́ков и ухо́да из Афганиста́на. (Р. Медве́дев «Андре́й Са́харов и Алекса́ндр Солжени́цын» 2002)

And he demands the release of the political prisoners and an exit from Afghanistan – attaboy! (Medvedev, *Andrey Sakharov and Alexander Solzhenitsyn*, 2002)

Всё-таки она́ – молодчи́на, подума́л он, не испуга́лась, не хвата́ла его́ за ру́ки и коле́ни в э́той безу́мной го́нке, не визжа́ла. (Д. Ру́бина «Бе́лая голу́бка Кордо́вы» 2009)

"And yet, she did good," he thought, "she wasn't scared, she didn't grab him by the arm or knee in that mad race, never squealed." (Rubina, *The White Dove of Cordoba*, 2009)

Како́й же ты Фёдор, молодча́га!

Attaboy, Fyodor!

Она́ молодчи́на, всё сдела́ет, как на́до, не растеря́ется.

She's smart, she'll do everything right, she won't lose her head.

50   *Entries*

Мудри́ла

Someone who over-intellectualizes and philosophizes. Used with irony.

Originates from the noun **му́дрость** *wisdom* and the verb **мудри́ть** *overthink*. The synonymous **у́мник** *smarty-pants* articulates less irony and more disapproval, and is used more often than **мудри́ла**. Often used with the verb **приду́мывать** *to make up* and the adjective **изве́стный** *renowned*.

Пётр Ива́нович, мудри́ла изве́стный, напридумывает, пото́м не разберёшься.	Pyotr Ivanovich is a renowned overthinker – he'll come up with something so convoluted that you won't be able to wrap your head around it.
Така́я мудри́ла э́та Ле́нка, опя́ть написа́ла тако́е, что никто́ не мо́жет поня́ть, что она́ име́ла в виду́.	That Lenka is such a brainiac – she wrote another piece, and nobody can figure out what she meant.
Ну ты и скажи́, ты же изве́стный мудри́ла.	Then *you* say something! You're the renowned thinker!

Мя́мля

An undetermined, hesitating, and unenergetic individual, or else someone who speaks slowly and indistinctly. Conveys contempt and disrespect.

The latter meaning is derived from the verb **мя́млить** *to mumble*. **Размазня́** is a synonym for the former meaning. The synonymous **ро́хля** additionally implies physical frailty.

See **размазня́, ро́хля**.

Но никто́ никогда́ не трактова́л Ко́лю как баскетболи́ста, а то́лько как мя́млю и тро́ечника . . . (А. На́йман «Сла́вный коне́ц бессла́вных поколе́ний» 1994)	But nobody ever regarded Kolya as a basketball player, they saw him only as a doormat and a C-student . . . (Nayman, *The Glorious End of Inglorious Generations*, 1994)

Entries 51

– Смотре́ть то́шно! Мя́мля! С ма́льчишкой спра́виться не мо́жет. . . (Д. Мережко́вский «Воскре́сшие Бо́ги. Леона́рдо да Ви́нчи» 1901)

"It's painful to watch! Sissy! Can't even take on a little boy . . ." (Merezhkovsky, *Resurrected Gods: Leonardo Da Vinci, 1901*)

Оказа́лся ваш судья́ больши́м мя́млей, тру́сом и подлецо́м.

Your judge turned out to be a great doormat, coward, and scoundrel.

Ну и нереши́тельная мя́мля же ты, А́лла, никогда́ за себя́ постоя́ть не мо́жешь.

Alla, you're such an indecisive sissy, you never stand up for yourself.

Неве́жа

A rude, impolite, and poorly mannered individual. Conveys disapproval and disrespect.

Derived from the adjective **неве́жливый** *rude*. Do not confuse **неве́жа** with the noun **неве́жда**.

See **неве́жда**.

Вспо́мнил, что сиде́л, как неве́жа, отверну́вшись от вас, извини́те. (К. Си́монов «Так называ́емая ли́чная жизнь» 1973)

I just remembered that I behaved like a boor, sitting with my back to you, my apologies. (Simonov, *The So-Called Private Life*, 1973)

Вы – ю́ный неве́жа. Вы позволя́ете себе́ перебива́ть ста́ршего во вре́мя разгово́ра.

You are a youthful boor. You permit yourself to interrupt your elder in conversation.

(Б. Лавренёв «Круше́ние респу́блики Итль» 1925)

(Lavrenyov, *The Destruction of the Republic of Itl'*, 1925)

От э́того грубия́на и невежи́ ждать хоро́ших мане́р не прихо́дится.

There's no reason to expect good manners from that smart-mouthed boor.

С тако́й невоспи́танной де́вочкой, неве́жей, уже́ давно́ не приходи́лось ста́лкиваться.

It's been a long time since I've met an ill-mannered boor of a little girl like you.

52   *Entries*

Неве́жда

An ignorant, uneducated person. Expresses contempt.

Derived from the adjective **неве́жественный** *ignorant* (which is more emphatic than **неве́жда**) and the noun **неве́жество** *ignorance*. Can combine with the adjectives **кру́глый** *round* and **по́лный** *utter*. Do not confuse **неве́жда** with the noun **неве́жа**. Semantically close to **недоу́чка**.

See **неве́жа, недоу́чка**.

Но он был безгра́мотен, не хоте́л учи́ться и, хотя́ свое́й суту́лостью и близору́костью сма́хивал на челове́ка образо́ванного, на са́мом де́ле был неве́жда. (А. Рыбако́в «Тяжёлый песо́к» 1978)

But he was illiterate, he didn't want to go to school, and although his slouch and nearsightedness gave him the air of an educated man, he was actually an ignoramus. (Rybakov, *Heavy Sand*, 1978)

Она́ прекра́сно гото́вила, а я и по сей день по́лная неве́жда в кулина́рной о́бласти. (Л. Верти́нская «Си́няя пти́ца любви́» 2004)

She cooked beautifully, while I am to this day an absolute ignoramus in the culinary sphere. (Vertinskaya, *The Blue Bird of Love*, 2004)

Наш преподава́тель так объясня́л, что са́мые тру́дные зада́чи станови́лись досту́пны любо́му неве́жде.

Our teacher explained things so well that even the most difficult problems became accessible to any ignoramus.

Э́того полно́го неве́жду не люби́ли не то́лько потому́, что он ничего́ не знал, но и потому́, что он уве́рен был, что зна́ет всё лу́чше всех.

Nobody liked that utter ignoramus not just because he did not know anything, but because he was confident that he knew everything better than anyone else.

Невиди́мка

Someone who is invisible. Used in many cases as an appositive clarifying another noun.

Entries 53

Derived from the adjective **невидимый** *invisible*. The common term **человек-невидимка** *invisible man* is used in different contexts and agrees with masculine words because of the masculine **человек** *man*. **Шапка-невидимка** *the hat of invisibility* is a common character in many fairy tales.

У него жена-невидимка –
то она есть, то её нет. . .
(М. Петросян «Дом, в
котором. . .» 2009)

He has a disappearing wife –
one minute she's there, the next
she's gone . . . (Petrosyan, *The
House Where . . .*, 2009)

Фотография была выполнена
настолько искусно и
качественно, что казалось,
будто невидимка фотограф
стоял на расстоянии вытянутой
руки. . . (Е. Сухов «Делу
конец – сроку начало» 2007)

The photo was done so artfully
and well that it seemed like the
phantom photographer stood
but an arm's length away . . .
(Sukhov, *The Job Ends – The
Term Begins*, 2007)

Наташа, снимавшая у них
комнату, была как невидимка
и никому не мешала.

It was as if Natasha, who was
renting one of their rooms, was
invisible – she didn't bother
anyone.

Сергей давно превратился
в человека- невидимку,
которого никто не замечал.

Sergey long ago had turned into
an invisible man, unnoticed by
all.

Недотёпа

A clumsy and inept individual, perhaps not very intelligent. Can pertain to someone's physical and mental attributes. Expresses pity.

In certain situations, it can be replaced with the noun **неумеха**, which focuses more on the fact that the person is unable to do anything well.

See **неумеха**.

Как же ты не сообразил,
недотёпа, что важное дело
государственной безопасности
не терпит гласности?
(П. Сиркес «Труба исхода» 1999)

You oaf, how did you not
realize that homeland security
doesn't allow for diversity of
opinion? (Sirkes, *The Horn of
Exodus*, 1999)

54   *Entries*

Он потешал класс
артистическими выходками,
играл под недотёпу-дурачка.
(Д. Каралис «Автопортрет»
1999)

He amused the class with artful
pranks and pretended to be a
foolish oaf. (Karalis, *A Self-
Portrait*, 1999)

Эх ты, какой недотёпа. Что ж
ты простую задачку решить
не можешь?

You poor oaf, can't solve even a
simple problem.

Простите его, недотёпу, всё
из рук валится – то чашку
разобьёт, то часы сломает.

Forgive him, he's a klutz,
everything falls out of his
hands, cups, clocks, everything.

Недотрога

Someone who is oversensitive and overdelicate. Easily and unreasonably offended, does not react to jokes at his/her expense well. Frequently used in situations when someone makes sexual advances. Conveys disapproval.

Derived from the verb **не дотронуться** *not to touch*. Associated with the word **мимоза**, which literally means the plant *mimosa*, but also means *shrinking violet*. The noun **неженка** can be a synonym. Can also be used to make the phrases **строить из себя недотрогу** *act like a prude* or **корчить из себя недотрогу** *act like a prude*. The latter sounds very rude and is low in terms of style.

See **неженка**.

Ох, уж этот недотрога
офицер, никакими бабьими
чарами его не купишь, он
бежит от неё, как монах от
нечистой силы. (В. Шишков
«Емельян Пугачёв» 1942)

That prudish officer is immune
to womanly charms – he runs
from her like a monk from
unholy spirits. (Shishkov,
Yemelyan Pugachev, 1942)

Если на ней не женишься, так
и за руку не держи! Скажите,
какая недотрога! (Г. Николаева
«Битва в пути» 1959)

If you don't marry her, don't
even think about touching her
hand! What a prude! (Nikolaeva,
A Battle on the Way, 1959)

Entries 55

Он, конéчно, срáзу нáчал к ней пристáвáть – для тогó и привёл, а онá решúла, что сопротивлялться не нýжно, потомý что ведь знáла, для чегó он её сюдá зовёт, и скóлько же мóжно стрóить из себя недотрóгу, рáди чегó, рáди когó? (А. Берсéнева «Полёт над разлýкой» 2007)

Naturally, he immediately began to make advances – it was why he brought her there, and she thought that she shouldn't resist, because she knew why he was calling her over, and how much longer could she act like a prude, for whom, for what reason? (Berseneva, *Flight Over a Separation*, 2007)

Уж и словá не скажú – кóрчит из себя недотрóгу, а сам когó угóдно обúдеть мóжет.

You can't say anything to the guy! He acts like a prude, but he himself is more than willing to make fun of others.

Недоýчка

Someone who has not completed their education and is only semi-educated. Conveys disapproval and disdain, but can also express empathy and understanding.

Derived from the verb **не доучúться** *not to finish one's education.* Semantically close to **невéжда**. Can be associated with the noun **простáк** *simpleton*. Frequently used as an appositive.

See **невéжда**.

. . . э́то ничтóжество, э́тот вы́скочка, дорвáвшийся до корóны чéрез гóлову брáта, э́тот недоýчка с амбúциями капрáла дóлжен прáвить мнóю, вáми?! (М. Шúшкин «Всех ожидáет однá ночь» 1993)

. . . that nonentity, that parvenu who clambered over his brother to get to the crown, that dropout with a corporal's ambitions is supposed to tell you and me what to do?! (Shishkin, *The Same Night Waits for Everyone*, 1993)

Девчóнка шестнáдцати лет, недоýчка- детдóмовка, оказáлась такúм óпытным проводникóм в незнáемое прекрáсное. (Г. Щербакóва «Áнгел Мёртвого óзера» // «Нóвый Мир» 2002)

A sixteen-year-old girl, a dropout from an orphanage, turned out to be such an experienced guide into the great unknown. (Shcherbakova, "The Angel of the Dead Lake," 2002)

. . . когда́ Никола́й вдруг узна́л, что я – недоу́чка и в како́й-то ме́ре скита́лец, бродя́га, то прони́кся ко мне и́скренним уваже́нием. (В. Бондаре́нко «Покая́ние гре́шного Гле́бушки . . .» // «Наш совреме́нник» 2003)	. . . when Nikolai suddenly found out that I'm a dropout and something of a vagabond, he developed a newfound, genuine sense of respect for me. (Bondarenko, "Wicked Glebushka's Repentance," 2003)
А Ю́ля, самоуве́ренная недоу́чка, счита́ет, что всё зна́ет лу́чше всех и ни с кем не сове́туется.	But Yulya, a cocky dropout, believes that she knows everything better than everyone else and doesn't listen to anyone.

Не́женка

A pushover. An oversensitive and possibly pampered person. Conveys disapproval or even disdain.

Derived from the adjective **не́жный** *delicate* and the noun **не́га** *luxury*. The adjective **впечатли́тельный** *impressionable*, as well as the nouns **белору́чка** and **сибари́т** *sybarite*, are close to **не́женка**. The noun **недотро́га** and the phrase **ма́менькин сыно́к** *momma's boy* are synonymous.

See **белору́чка**, **недотро́га**.

Всё здесь не по нём, – гова́ривал он, – за столо́м привере́дничает, не ест, людско́го за́паху, духоты́ переноси́ть не мо́жет, вид пья́ных его́ расстра́ивает, дра́ться при нём то́же не смей, служи́ть не хоче́т: слаб, вишь, здоро́вьем; фу ты, не́женка э́дакой! (И. Турге́нев «Дворя́нское гнездо́» 1859)	"Nothing suits him," he would say, "he's picky at the table, he doesn't eat, he hates how others smell, he can't stand humidity, he's upset by the sight of drunks, don't even think about fighting in his presence: his health isn't very good, you see: bah, what a sissy!" (Turgenev, *Home of the Gentry*, 1959)

Он был не́женка. Он так
боя́лся бо́ли, что при
мале́йшем несча́стье замира́л,
ничего́ не предпринима́л, а всё
наде́ялся на лу́чшее. (Е. Шварц
«Обыкнове́нное чу́до» 1956)

He was a pushover. He was so
afraid of pain that he froze at
the slightest misfortune, did
nothing, and hoped for the
best. (Schwartz, *An Ordinary
Miracle*, 1956)

Не люби́ли его́ за то, что
дра́ться не уме́л, был
ужа́сным не́женкой и
ма́менькиным сынко́м.

People disliked him, because
he couldn't fight and was
an unbearable sissy and a
momma's boy.

На́стя, не́женка, ви́дите ли
в авто́бусе мно́го люде́й,
толка́ются, поэ́тому сиди́т
до́ма и е́хать никуда́ не
хо́чет – маши́ну ей подава́й.

See, there are a lot of people in
the bus, pushing and shoving,
which is why Nastya, that sissy,
is sitting at home, not wanting
to go anywhere – only a private
car for her!

Незна́йка

Someone who knows very little. In contemporary Russian, **незна́йка**
is associated with the character from Nikolai Nosov's children's
book *Know-Nothing*. Typically refers to children.

Derived from the verb **не знать** *not to know*.

Она́ ти́хо усну́ла в мои́х
рука́х, ма́ленькая незна́йка.
(И. Шмелёв «Со́лнце
мёртвых» 1923)

She quietly fell asleep in my
arms, the little know-nothing.
(Shmelev, *The Sun of the Dead*,
1923)

Успоко́йся, никто́ тебя́,
тёмного незна́йку, и
слу́шать-то не бу́дет.

Relax, nobody's going to listen
to an ignorant dunce like you.

Незна́йка мой, пора́ уже́
взросле́ть и знать таки́е ве́щи.

My little dunce, it's about time to
grow up and know these things.

Оте́ц пошёл укла́дывать свою́
люби́мую незна́йку.

The father went to put his
favorite know-nothing to sleep.

58 *Entries*

Непосе́да

A very energetic person, someone who is full of activity, incapable of staying in one place, and travels a lot. Typically refers to children, but can also be directed at adults.

Derived from the adjective **непосе́дливый** *restless*. Semantically close to **его́за**.

See **его́за**.

Была́ непосе́да, до́ма вре́мени проводи́ла ма́ло, в основно́м на у́лице, с подру́жками, с ребя́тами. (Т. Шмы́га «Сча́стье мне улыба́лось. . .» 2000)	She was a restless spirit – she spent little time at home, instead spending it outside, with her girlfriends, with the guys. (Shmyga, *Fortune Smiled at Me*, 2000)
Втора́я на́ша дочь Татья́на родила́сь 19 апре́ля 1988 го́да на ме́сяц ра́ньше сро́ка. Она́ и сейча́с така́я непосе́да. (С. Спивако́ва «Не всё» 2002)	Our second daughter, Tatyana, was born on April 19, 1988, a month early. She's still the same eager beaver. (Spivakova, *Not Everything*, 2002)
Мла́дший Андре́й был непосе́да, бе́гал по луга́м, по ле́су, собира́л плоды́ шипо́вника и т.п. (С. Капи́ца «Мои́ воспомина́ния» 2008)	Andrei, the younger kid, was a restless child – he ran around the fields, gathered rosehip, etc. (Kapitsa, *My Memories*, 2008)
Серге́й никогда́ не сиде́л на ме́сте, всегда́ был непосе́дой и объе́здил весь мир.	Sergei never sat in one place – he was always a restless spirit and travelled around the whole world.

Неро́вня

Someone who is different from or unequal to others socially, physically, mentally, or in some other way. Mainly used in contemporary Russian in the nominative case.

Derived from the adjective **неро́вный** *uneven*. Synonymous with phrases **кто-то кому́-то не па́ра/не чета́** *someone is no match for*

Entries 59

someone. **Не па́ра** is stylistically neutral, while **не чета́** is elevated. Antonymous with **ро́вня**.

See **ро́вня**.

Иногда́ э́то мотиви́руется тем, что геро́й – солда́т и́ли мужи́к, и что он неро́вня царе́вне. (В. Пропп «Истори́ческие ко́рни волше́бной ска́зки» 1946)	Sometimes this is motivated by the fact that the hero is a soldier or a farmer, in no way the tsarevna's equal. (Propp, *Historical Roots of Fairy Tales*, 1946)
Но Бы́чин, хотя́ и надува́ется, как павли́н, а всё же понима́ет ра́зумом: Шу́ра ему́ неро́вня, он в па́ртии полтора́ го́да, а Шу́ра – пятна́дцать лет. (Ю. Три́фонов «Стари́к» 1978)	But even though he puffs up like a peacock, Bychin understands that he and Shura are not equals – he's been in the party for a year and a half, while she's been in it for fifteen years. (Trifonov, *Old Man*, 1978)
Неро́вня она́ тебе́ – взгля́ды, запро́сы и привы́чки други́е, а гла́вное – се́мьи ва́ши из ра́зного те́ста.	She is not your equal – your views, your demands, your habits are all different, and most importantly, your families are cut from completely different cloths.
Маргари́та ему́ была́ неро́вня, и она́ всегда́ э́то чу́вствовала.	They were never on a level playing field, and Margarita was always aware of it.

Неря́ха

An untidy individual. Expresses disapproval and disdain.

Originates from the adjective **неря́шливый** *sloven*. The synonymous **неаккура́тный челове́к** *an untidy person* is stylistically neutral. Semantically close to **грязну́ля** and **замара́шка**, which express positive feelings and are typically used to refer to children. Synonymous with **растрёпа** which focuses more often on untidy hair. **Аккура́тный челове́к** *a tidy person* is an antonym. Also antonymous with **чисту́ля**.

See **грязну́ля, замара́шка, растрёпа, чисту́ля**.

60   *Entries*

Я ви́жу, что вы, молодо́й челове́к, неря́ха, не лю́бите зу́бы чи́стить. (Е. Чару́шин «Тю́па, То́мка и соро́ка» 1946)	I see that you, young man, are a slob, you do not like to brush your teeth. (Charushin, *Tyupa, Tomka, and the Magpie*, 1946)
А сама́ неуме́лая, неря́ха – всё у неё вали́лось из рук. (И. Гре́кова «Под фонарём» 1963)	She herself was inept, a hot mess – she managed to drop everything she held. (Grekova, *Beneath the Lamppost*, 1963)
Ста́лину в Ха́рьков: «Пригрози́те расстре́лом э́тому неря́хе, кото́рый, заве́дуя свя́зью, не уме́ет дать Вам хоро́шего усили́теля и доби́ться по́лной испра́вности телефо́нной свя́зи со мной». (В. Ерофе́ев «Моя́ ма́ленькая лениниа́на» 1988)	To Stalin in Kharkiv: "Threaten that slob with execution if, being in charge of communications, he is unable to get you a good boosting device and restore our telephone connection." (Yerofeev, *My Little Leniniana*, 1988)
Что де́лать с э́тим неря́хой?! В ко́мнате грязь. Ве́щи не пости́раны и валя́ются везде́.	What to do about that slob?! The room is filthy. His dirty things are strewn around everywhere.

Неуме́йка

Someone who does not know how to do something. Typically used with humor to address children.

Derived from the verb **не уме́ть** *not to know how to do something*. Synonymous with **неуме́ха**, which places a greater emphasis on one's laziness and is typically used to refer to adults and usually expresses scorn.

See **неуме́ха**.

Кака́я-то неуме́йка – да́же просто́й суп свари́ть не мо́жет.	She's some kind of nonstarter – she can't even make soup.
Э́тому неуме́йке ничего́ поручи́ть нельзя́ – всё равно́ не сде́лает.	You can't tell that nonstarter to do anything – he just won't do it.

У нас но́вый нача́льник. Хоть уже́ и с о́пытом, но, ка́жется, что неуме́йка.

We have a new boss. He has experience, but he seems like a nonstarter.

Дед всегда́ помога́ет ма́ленькому неуме́йке вну́ку смастери́ть пода́рок кому́-нибудь.

Grandpa is always helping his nonstarter grandson improvise a present for someone.

Неуме́ха (неумёха)

Someone who is inept at doing things or who does not have the necessary skills or experience. Conveys disapproval, but can also express pity.

Derived from the verb **не уме́ть** *not to know how to do something* and the adjective **неуме́лый** *inept*. **Неуме́ха** is associated with laziness. Synonymous with **неуме́йка**, which is more humorous and typically used to address children. In certain situations, it can be replaced with the noun **недотёпа**.

See **недотёпа**, **неуме́йка**.

Неуме́ха, ду́ра, что ты уме́ешь в жи́зни, кро́ме как подгля́дывать, подслу́шивать и рисова́ть каля́ки-маля́ки, над кото́рыми смею́тся роди́тели. (Г. Щербако́ва «Ма́льчик и де́вочка» 2001)

You silly, unskilled fool, what do you know how to do in life other than spy and eavesdrop and draw scribbles that make your parents laugh? (Shcherbakova, *A Boy and a Girl*, 2001)

Потому́ что не узна́л бы, что она́ така́я неуме́ха, что котле́т не мо́жет нажа́рить, варе́нья свари́ть – вообще́ хозя́йства вести́. (М. Ку́черская «Тётя Мо́тя» // «Зна́мя» 2012)

Because I wouldn't have learned that she was so incompetent, that she can't make cutlets or jam or generally maintain a household. (Kucherskaya, "Aunt Motya," 2012)

Надое́ло рабо́тать за э́ту неуме́ху Никола́я. Непоня́тно, чему́ его́ то́лько в институ́те учи́ли.

I'm tired of working for that bushleaguer, Nikolai. Did they manage to teach him *anything* at that institute of his?

В отличие от отца, который умница и умел делать всё, он был неумеха и недотёпа.

Unlike his father, who knew how to do everything, he was a klutz.

Нюня

Someone who cries, moans, and complains unreasonably often. Conveys disapproval and disdain. Frequently refers to children. Can also indicate someone, usually an adult, who is a weakling.

The synonymous **плакса** expresses less negativity. Can be synonymous with **размазня**. The phrase **распускать нюни** *snivel* is frequently used. Semantically close to **рёва**.

See **плакса**, **размазня**, **рёва**.

Ничто не могло прогнать кислого выражения на её лице, и самая улыбка была такая, что другому невольно становилось досадно, и он думал про себя: «Вот нюня противная!» (3. Гиппиус «Без талисмана» 1896)

Nothing could wipe the sour expression from her face, and her very smile made others inadvertently think: "Good god, what a ninny!" (Gippius, *Without a Talisman*, 1896)

Успокойся, истеричка, нюня, чепуховый человечишко! Успокойся, иначе ты совершенно никому не будешь нужен! (Ю. Герман «Дорогой мой человек» 1961)

Calm down, you hysterical crybaby, you silly little human! Calm down, or no one will have any use for you! (German, *My Dear Man*, 1961)

Эх ты, нюня! Нюня и плакса. Что ты хнычешь? Кого испугался?! Он же младше и слабее тебя.

You ninny! A ninny and a crybaby. What are you sniveling about? Who are you afraid of?! He's younger and weaker than you!

Роман Иванович никогда постоять за себя не сможет – нюня он и размазня.

Roman Ivanovich could never stand up for himself – he was a ninny.

Обжо́ра

A glutton. Someone who eats large amounts of food nonstop. Conveys a strongly negative attitude and expresses disapproval and disdain. Sounds very rude. At the same time, can be used humorously.

Derived from the adjective **обжо́рливый** *gluttonous* and the verb **обжира́ться** *to pig out*. Its synonym **объеда́ла** is used less frequently and sounds less rude, but also strongly expresses disapproval.

See **объеда́ла**.

Он же – обжо́ра, а не знато́к, поглоща́л всё, что Кса́на в таре́лку подкла́дывала. (Н. Ко́жевникова «В лёгком жа́нре» 1986)	But he was a glutton, not a connoisseur, and he devoured everything Ksana put on his plate. (Kozhevnikova, *In a Light Genre*, 1986)
Э́тот пья́ница, кури́льщик, ба́бник, обжо́ра, гуля́ка – мой ста́рший брат. (Б. Ефи́мов «Де́сять десятиле́тий» 2000)	That boozehound, smoker, womanizer, glutton, and drunk is my older brother. (Yefimov, *Ten Decades*, 2000)
Пошёл к ры́нку, купи́л себе́ четы́ре хот-до́га и все их тут же съел. Го́споди, прости́ меня́, гре́шного и обжо́ру. (М. Куче́рская «Совреме́нный патери́к: чте́ние для впа́вших в уны́ние» 2004)	I went to the market, bought four hot dogs, and ate them all there and then. May God have mercy on my sinful, gluttonous soul. (Kucherskaya, *A Modern Patericon: Reading for The Despondent*, 2004)
Все с презре́нием относи́лись к э́той обжо́ре и обходи́ли её стороно́й.	Everyone despised that glutton, and they all steered clear of her.

Объеда́ла

Someone who eats a lot and is incapable of stopping. Expresses negative emotions, disapproval, and scorn. Sounds rude.

Derived from the verb **объеда́ться** *to gorge oneself* and sounds less rude and is used less often than the synonymous **обжо́ра**.

See **обжо́ра**.

64 *Entries*

Взгляни́те на высо́кого человека в поно́шеном кафта́не: э́то объеда́ла. (Н. Карамзи́н «Волшебно́й фона́рь и́ли карти́на Пари́жа» // «Ве́стник Евро́пы» 1802)

Look at the tall man in the worn kaftan – he is a voracious eater. (Karamzin, "The Magical Lamp, or a Portrait of Paris," 1802)

То́лько тако́й болва́н, как я, мог поле́зть на инжи́р с корзи́ной, когда́ э́та объеда́ла стои́т под де́ревом и при э́том ни на мину́ту не замолка́ет. (Ф. Исканде́р «Сандро́ из Чеге́ма» 1989)

Only a moron like me could have made for the figs with that glutton standing under the tree, not shutting up even for a minute. (Iskander, *Sandro of Chegem*, 1989)

Бы́стро ешь. Придёт объеда́ла Лю́да и тебе́ ничего́ не доста́нется.

Eat fast. That glutton Lyuda is on her way – there'll be nothing left.

Одино́чка

A loner. Someone who lives or acts alone without anybody's help. Often used as an appositive to clarify another noun and predominantly used in the nominative case. Can convey negative or positive emotions, depending on the situation.

The following noun-appositive combinations are commonly used in discourse: **мать-одино́чка** *lone mother*, **оте́ц-одино́чка** *lone father*, **уби́йца-одино́чка** *lone killer*, **волк-одино́чка** (figuratively and literally) *lone wolf*, **куста́рь-одино́чка** *lone craftsman*, etc.

Смотри́, ведь что он наду́мал, зате́йник: топи́ть котёнка. Куста́рь-одино́чка, одержи́мый ме́стью. (Д. Ру́бина «Ру́сская канаре́йка. Блу́дный сын» 2014)

Look at what he's come up with, the joker: he wants to drown the cat. A lone craftsman, blinded by vengeance. (Rubina, *Russian Canary. The Prodigal Son*, 2014)

Он был закорене́лый одино́чка, и его́ нево́льно уважа́ли, мо́жет, кто и недолю́бливал за

He was an inveterate loner, and he was grudgingly respected. Some may have disliked his

обосо́бленность от люде́й, но уважа́ли. (В. Реми́зов «Во́ля во́льная» // «Но́вый мир» 2013)

detachment from others, but respected him nonetheless. (Remizov, "Willful Will," 2013)

Она́ по свое́й нату́ре одино́чка. Она́ сама́ никому́ не нужна́, но и ей никто́ не ну́жен.

She's a loner by her nature. Nobody needs her, but she doesn't need anybody either.

Отцу́-одино́чке самому́ тру́дно вы́растить и воспита́ть трои́х дете́й.

It is difficult for a lone father to raise three kids.

Па́инька

Someone who is obedient and well-behaved. Expresses fondness and tenderness because of the diminutive suffix **-иньк-**. However, it can also be disrespectful.

Commonly used in the phrase **будь па́инька** *be on your best behavior*. Frequently used in combination with the noun **у́мница**. The synonyms **пай-ма́льчик** *good little boy* and **пай-де́вочка** *good little girl* might convey condescension. Can be a synonym for **тихо́ня**.

See **тихо́ня, у́мница**.

А гля́нешь на тебя́ – така́я скро́мница, така́я па́инька! (А. Берсе́нева «Во́зраст тре́тьей любви́» 2005)

But take one look at you, and it's clear you're so modest, such a goody-two-shoes. (Berseneva, *The Age of the Third Love*, 2005)

Па́па лежа́л в гробу́, сложи́в ру́ки, как пай́нька. (М. Ши́шкин «Письмо́вник» // «Зна́мя» 2010)

Daddy lay in his coffin, arms folded, like a little angel. (Shishkin, "The Letter-Writer," 2010)

Мы ухо́дим, а ты будь у́мницей и па́инькой и веди́ себя́ хорошо́.

We're leaving – while we're gone, be an angel and behave.

Э́тот пай-ма́льчик, э́тот па́инька, не в состоя́нии самостоя́тельно принима́ть взро́слые реше́ния.

That good little boy is incapable of making adult decisions on his own.

66 *Entries*

Писа́ка

A bad writer; someone who writes often, but poorly. Scornful and disrespectful.

Derived from the verb **писа́ть**.

Как хоти́те, а ведь его́ статьи́ служи́ли украше́нием столбцо́в распространённого литерату́рного о́ргана, а совсе́м плохо́му писа́ке така́я роль не под си́лу. (М. Салтыко́в-Щедри́н «Пёстрые пи́сьма» 1884)

Believe what you want, but his articles decorated the columns of a well-known literary organization, and a bona fide hack couldn't make that happen. (Saltykov-Shchedrin, *Colorful Letters*, 1884)

Ви́дно, что э́тот газе́тный писа́ка не смы́слит в вое́нно-морско́м де́ле ни у́ха ни ры́ла. (А. Но́виков-Прибо́й «Цуси́ма» 1932)

It's clear that this hack of a journalist doesn't know a single thing about maritime war. (Novikov-Priboy, *Tsushima*, 1932)

Писа́л-то её писа́ка, а вдохновля́л и приду́мывал совсе́м друго́й челове́к, и да́же не оди́н, а це́лая соли́дная компа́ния. (Ю. Три́фонов «Утоле́ние жа́жды» 1966)

It was written by a hack, but it was inspired by someone completely different, even by *someones* completely different, a whole company. (Trifonov, *Quenching the Thirst*, 1966)

Мы не могли́ примири́ться с нечистопло́тностью кинокри́тика и реши́ли наказа́ть писа́ку, разоблачи́ть его́, схвати́ть за ру́ку. (Э. Ряза́нов «Подведённые ито́ги» 2005)

We couldn't accept the film critic's dishonesty and decided to teach the hack a lesson, expose him, bust him. (Ryazanov, *The Bottom Line*, 2005)

Пла́кса

A crybaby. Someone who cries often and without a good reason. Primarily conveys disapproval, but can sound sympathetic. Frequently used to refer to children.

Entries 67

Derived from the verb **пла́кать** *to cry*. Semantically close to **капризу́ля**. The synonymous **ню́ня** additionally indicates someone who whines and moans a lot, while the synonymous **рёва** expresses more negativity. The phrase **пла́кса-ва́кса** *sissy* is used to tease.

See **капризу́ля, ню́ня, рёва**.

А я о́чень не люблю́, когда́ ви́дят, как я пла́чу. Я во́все не пла́кса, пове́рьте мне! (Е. Шварц «Сне́жная короле́ва» 1938)	I don't like it at all when people see me crying. I'm not a crybaby, believe me! (Schwartz, *The Ice Queen*, 1938)
Я поняла́, что должна́ уе́хать, – сего́дня, я запла́чу ра́ньше вре́мени, я же пла́кса. (Д. Ру́бина «Ру́сская канаре́йка. Блу́дный сын» 2014)	I've realized that I have to leave – today, right now . . . Wait, let me get it out, or . . . or I'll start crying prematurely, I'm a crybaby, after all. (Rubina, *Russian Canary. The Prodigal Son*, 2014)
Ну что ты раскапри́зничался? Пла́кса ты э́такая. Переста́нь пла́кать и иди́ умо́йся.	What are you crying about? You crybaby. Stop crying and go wash up.

Побиру́шка

A beggar. Expresses sympathy, but can also articulate disapproval and condemnation.

Derived from the verb **побира́ться** *to beg*. The synonymous **попроша́йка** conveys more negativity. Semantically close to the word **ни́щий** *destitute*.

See **попроша́йка**.

Э́та побиру́шка ходи́ла под о́кнами и ро́бко проси́ла ми́лостыню . . . (А. Гайда́р «Пусть све́тит» 1933)	That beggar meandered beneath the windows and timidly begged alms . . . (Gaidar, *Let It Shine*, 1933)
Де́нег, сла́ва бо́гу, скопи́л, не ни́щий челове́к, не побиру́шка тесть у тебя́. (Ю. Ге́рман «Росси́я молода́я» 1952)	I've saved up enough money, thank God, I'm not destitute, your father-in-law isn't some beggar. (German, *Young Russia*, 1952)

Жа́лкая неуда́чница, побиру́шка, живу́щая на кро́хи от чужо́й уда́чи и предусмотри́тельности. (П. Аки́мов «Пла́та за страх» 2000)

A pitiful failure, a beggar, living off the crumbs of others' fortune and forethought. (Akimov, *The Wages of Fear*, 2000)

В рука́х у него́ была́ таре́лка с густы́м морски́м су́пом. Ви́дно, кто-то угости́л популя́рного побиру́шку. (В. Аксёнов «Но́вый сла́достный стиль» 2005)

He had in his hands a bowl of thick seafood soup. Someone had evidently given the popular beggar a treat. (Aksyonov, *A Delightful New Style*, 2005)

Подли́за

A brown noser. Someone who acts very obsequiously around others, currying favor by flattering or pleasing them. Conveys strong disdain and contempt.

Derived from the verb **подли́зываться** *to suck up*. The synonymous **подхали́м** *toady* is less conversational, while **подлипа́ла** is less common. Semantically close to **подпева́ла**.

See **подлипа́ла, подпева́ла**.

Меня́ постоя́нно хвали́ли за приме́рное поведе́ние, а това́рищи называ́ли за э́то «подли́зой». (А. Осипо́вич (Новодво́рский) «Карье́ра» 1880)

People constantly praised me for my exemplary behavior, which made my buddies call me a brown noser. (Osipovich (Novodvorsky), *Career*, 1880)

И часте́нько получа́лось, что уме́лый подли́за, несмотря́ на свою́ безда́рность, аж сгиба́лся под тя́жестью орденов и меда́лей, вися́щих на обо́их ла́цканах пиджака́. (Э. Ряза́нов «Подведённые ито́ги» 2005)

And it was often the case that despite his mediocrity, the skilled brown noser was bowed down by the weight of the medals that hung on both lapels of his jacket. (Ryazanov, *The Bottom Line*, 2005)

Наш учи́тель фи́зики терпе́ть не мог подли́з, и е́сли

Our physics professor couldn't stand brown nosers, and if

кто́-то подли́зывался, ста́вил
дво́йку.

anyone even tried to suck up to
him, he gave them a D.

Подлипа́ла

The same as **подли́за**. A brown noser. Someone who acts very
obsequiously around others, currying favor by flattering or pleasing
them. Conveys strong disdain and contempt.

Derived from the verb **ли́пнуть** *to stick*. The synonymous **подхали́м**
toady is less conversational, while **подли́за** is more common.
Semantically close to **подпева́ла**.

See **подли́за, подпева́ла**.

И тут, как наро́чно, мне
подверну́лась А́лла
Рожде́ственская. . . . Тёмная
ба́ба, ме́лкая авантюри́стка
и подлипа́ла, держи́тесь от
неё пода́льше. (Ю. Наги́бин
«Дневни́к» 1977)

And suddenly, as if on purpose,
Alla Rozhdestvenskaya appeared
out of nowhere. . . . A foolish
broad, a small-time schemer
and toady; keep away from her.
(Nagibin, *The Diary*, 1977)

Бы́вший неме́цкий подлипа́ла
вско́ре и здесь стал вась-вась
со всей лагобслу́гой и
сли́шком ча́сто спал в рабо́чее
вре́мя, е́сли то́лько не распева́л
пе́ред свои́ми покрови́телями.
(Г. Деми́дов «Лю́ди ги́бнут за
мета́лл» 1972–1980)

The former German toady
soon got in real good with the
camp workers and far too often
slept during working hours, if
only he wasn't singing for his
protectors. (Demidov, *People
Die for Metal*, 1972–1980)

Подлипа́ла: сде́лавший
карье́ру сни́зу, прислу́живая
тяну́вшему его́ за собо́й
хозя́ину. (М. Ве́ллер «Карье́ра
в Никуда́» 1988)

A toady: he built his career
from the bottom, serving his
master, who pulled him after
him. (Veller, *A Career to
Nowhere*, 1988)

Подлю́ка (подлю́га)

An offensive word that indicates a nasty, dishonorable person. Articulates strong negative feelings.

70   *Entries*

Derived from and is more emphatic than the adjective **по́длый** *low* and the noun **подле́ц** *scoundrel*. Synonymous with **мерза́вец** *bastard*.

Вот ты где, подлю́ка? Ах ты бандю́га, ах ты фаши́ст прокля́тый!. . (Н. Ду́бов «Не́бо с овчи́нку» 1966)	There you are, you bastard! You bandit, you damn fascist!. . (Dubov, *The Condensed Sky*, 1966)
Впро́чем, как сказа́л Ге́нрих, жена́ его́ была́ подлю́га и хорошо́, что Вади́м Па́влович с ней развяза́лся. (А. Рыбако́в «Тяжёлый песо́к» 1978)	Admittedly, as Henrich said, his wife was a nasty piece of work, and it was a good thing that Vadim Pavlovich parted ways with her. (Rybakov, *Heavy Sand*, 1978)
Спит – храпи́т, котле́ты жа́рить не уме́ет, всё че́рез коле́нку, а кварти́ра на нас двои́х тепе́рь запи́сана, свой ли́чный счёт, подлю́га, вы́правила. (И. Гре́кова «Перело́м» 1987)	She snores when she sleeps, she doesn't know how to make cutlets, everything is done haphazardly, but the apartment is now in both of our names – she's straightened out her own account, the snake. (Grekova, *The Fracture*, 1987)
Зна́чит, переигра́л меня́, подлю́га, – прохрипе́л банди́т, – чего́ же ждёшь, стреля́й! (Л. Дворе́цкий «Шака́лы» 2000)	"So you've beaten me, you bastard," the bandit croaked. "What are you waiting for, shoot me!" (Dvoretsky, *Jackals*, 2000)

Подпева́ла[1]

A backup singer. Stylistically neutral. Rarely used in contemporary language.

Derived from the verb **подпева́ть**, which literally means *to sing along*.

У неё само́й го́лос был неси́льный, поэ́тому была́ подпева́лой.	She herself didn't have a powerful voice, so she was a backup singer.

Уже́ пришли́ все: и музыка́нты, и подпева́лы, и уча́стники хо́ра.

Everyone's already here: the musicians, the backup singers, the choir members.

Подпева́ла²

Someone who sucks up to and fawns over others. Conveys disdain and contempt.

Derived from the verb **подпева́ть** *to sing along*, which figuratively means *to suck up*. Semantically close to **подли́за** and **подлипа́ла**.

See **подли́за**, **подлипа́ла**.

По ви́ду и ты колхо́зник, а на де́ле – кула́цкий подпева́ла. (М. Шо́лохов «По́днятая целина́» 1959)

You look like a farmer too, but in reality, you're a kulak toady. (Sholokhov, *Virgin Soil Upturned*, 1959)

Ви́дно, он намека́л на то, что Ря́бов – зубри́ла и остря́к-подпева́ла. (В. Железнико́в «Ка́ждый мечта́ет о соба́ке» 1966)

It was clear that he hinted that Ryabov was a rote memorizer and a deft suck-up. (Zheleznikov, *Everyone Dreams of Dogs*, 1966)

Он был сплéтник, я́бедник и подпева́ла. Он трево́жно и у́мно высма́тривал, что мне нра́вится, и хвали́л то́лько э́то. (Н. Саду́р «Не́мец» 1996)

He was a gossip, a snitch, and a toady. He restlessly and smartly discovered what I liked and praised only that. (Sadur, *The German*, 1996)

Приведи́те сюда́ э́ту подпева́лу, мо́жет, она́ расска́жет, что там бы́ло.

Bring that toady over here, maybe she'll tell us what happened.

Попроша́йка

A beggar or a tramp. Someone who begs for alms importunately. Articulates a strong negative overtone.

Derived from the verb **попрошáйничать** *to beg*. The synonymous **побирýшка** conveys less negativity and may express sympathy. Can be a synonym for **нúщий** *destitute*.

See **побирýшка**.

Попрошáйка-пьянчýжка был человéк совсéм сквéрный, бýйный и льстúвый. . . (Ф. Достоéвский «Господúн Прохáрчин» 1846)	The drunkard beggar was an utterly hateful, rowdy, and adulatory individual. (Dostoevsky, *Mister Prokharchin*, 1846)
Долговязая старýха, продолжáя шáркать вокрýг, гудéла жáлобно: Я не приживáлка, не попрошáйка какáя-нибудь. У меня свой дом. (Ю. Трúфонов «Дóлгое прощáние» 1971)	Continuing to shuffle around, the old woman buzzed pitifully, "I'm not a freeloader, not a beggar. I have my own home." (Trifonov, *A Long Farewell*, 1971)
Вóзле машúны стоял попрошáйка. – Дяденька, дáйте дéнег! (Ф. Искандéр «Поэт» // «Нóвый мир» 1998)	A beggar stood next to the car. "Mister, spare some money!" (Iskander, "The Poet," 1998)
Старúк-попрошáйка всё ещё околáчивался в темнотé у непристýпной двéри. (А. Снегирёв «Зúмние прáздники» // «Знáмя» 2012)	The old beggar still hung around in the darkness next to the impregnable door. (Snegiryov, "Winter Holidays," 2012)

Почемýчка

Someone who asks too many questions. Typically refers to children. Conveys a playful, joking overtone.

Derived from the question word **почемý** *why*.

Андрю́ша, ты мáленький почемýчка. Задаёшь одни и те же вопрóсы без перерыва.	Andryusha, you're just full of questions. You ask the same things over and over nonstop.
Это хорошó, когдá ребёнок почемýчка. Это знáчит, что он развивáется.	It's a good thing when a kid asks a lot of questions. That means he's developing.

Táня, бýдучи почемýчкой, задавáла вопрóсы не взрóслым, а кнѝгам.

Being a curious little girl, Tanya asked her questions not to adults, but to books.

Привере́да

Someone who is very picky, selective, and difficult to please. Expresses disapproval.

Derived from the verb **привере́дничать** *to be picky* and the adjective **привере́дливый** *picky*. Semantically close to **капризу́ля**.

See **капризу́ля**.

Мы еди́м то́лько куропáток с трюфеля́ми и шампиньо́ны . . . Привере́да ты, вот что! (А. Члéнов «Как Алёшка жил на Сéвере» 1978)

We eat only partridge with truffles and mushrooms. . . . You're a snob, you know that? (Chlenov, *How Alyoshka Lived in the North*, 1978)

. . . Кудáсов, уж на что был гурмáн и привере́да, а и тот, увлечённый азáртом Андре́я Ивáновича, однó за другѝм проглáтывал я́йца вкрутýю. (В. Орлóв «Альтѝст Данѝлов» 1980)

. . . Kudasov was a gourmand and a food snob, but even he, caught up in Andrey Ivanovich's fervor, swallowed hard-boiled eggs one after another. (Orlov, *Danilov, the Violist*, 1980)

Какáя же ты, Антóн, привере́да – всё не по тебé – и э́то не то, и э́то не так.

Anton, you're such a snob – this isn't to your liking, that isn't either.

Придѝра

Someone who finds faults and flaws in everything and vociferously condemns them all. Conveys disapproval, but can also be respectful.

Derived from the verb **придирáться** *to find faults* and the adjective **придѝрчивый** *hypercritical*. Semantically close to **крѝтик** *critic*.

И вся́кий, кто хóчет трудѝться инáче, – скандалѝст, придѝра, человéк с воспоминáниями

And anyone who wants to work another way is a troublemaker, a nitpicker, someone who

о том, что бы́ло при царе́ Горо́хе. (Г. Ко́зинцев «Тут начина́ется уже́ не хроноло́гия, но эпо́ха . . .» 1940–1973)

remembers what it was like under Tsar Gorokh. (Kozintsev, *Here Begins not a Chronology, but an Epoch. . .*, 1940–1973)

Да, приди́ра Марша́к иногда́ до слёз доводи́л нас свои́ми ненасы́тными тре́бованиями, но каки́е что ни день он сочиня́л эпигра́ммы! (Л. Чуко́вская «Про́черк» 2001)

Yes, Marshak, that nitpicker, sometimes drove us to tears with his insatiable requests, but he wrote such epigrams every day! (Chukovskaya, *The Strikethrough*, 2001)

Тут уж ни оди́н приди́ра, актёр или помре́ж, не в си́лах бы́ли угляде́ть слабины́, небре́жности и́ли игры́ «вполси́лы». (В. Сме́хов «Теа́тр мое́й па́мяти» 2001)

Not a single nitpicker, actor, or stage manager, was able to pick out weakness, carelessness, or "half-strength" acting. (Smekhov, *The Theater of My Memories*, 2011)

На на́ше несча́стье но́вая фи́зичка была́ моло́денькая и приди́ра ужа́сная – полови́на кла́сса схлопота́ла дво́йки на пе́рвом же уро́ке.

To our misfortune, the new physics teacher was young and very nitpicky – half the class earned themselves Ds the very first class.

Прилипа́ла

Someone who clings to somebody else and is impossible to get rid of or chase away. Expresses irritation and disdain.

Derived from the verb **прилипа́ть** *to stick*. Synonymous with **пристава́ла**, but conveys more negativity and annoyance.

See **пристава́ла**.

От Сла́вки не так легко́ отде́латься, он прилипа́ла, хотя́ и ханы́гой его́ не назовёшь. (Э. Лимо́нов «Подро́сток Са́венко» 1982)

Slavka is impossible to get rid of, he's a barnacle, though you can't call him a boozehound. (Limonov, *Savenko the Teen*, 1982)

Же́нька была́ прилипа́ла и никогда́ не понима́ла, что её

Zhen'ka was a clinger and never understood that her

присутствие мо́жет кому́-то не нра́вится.

presence might not be to everyone's liking.

Вот прилипа́ла – как ни гони́ его́, всё равно́ не отвя́жется.

He's such a barnacle – chase him away with all your might, but he just won't leave.

Пристава́ла

Someone who is clingy and impossible to get rid of. Possibly someone who makes sexual advances. Expresses irritation and disdain.

Derived from the verb **пристава́ть** *to stick, to hit on*. In its first meaning, synonymous with **прилипа́ла**, which conveys a little bit more negativity and annoyance.

See **прилипа́ла**.

На́до сказа́ть, что капита́н по́сле пе́рвых мои́х слов, уясни́в, что я не како́й-то там пристава́ла, отнёсся ко мне благоду́шно. (Ф. Исканде́р «Письмо́» 1969)

I have to say that after my first words, the captain realized that I wasn't some clinger and adopted a good-natured attitude towards me. (Iskander, *The Letter*, 1969)

. . . Кара́ев со свои́ми расска́зами похо́ж на пристава́лу, не понима́ющего, что его́ не хотя́т, что он отврати́телен и вызыва́ет лишь дрожь омерзе́ния. (В. Пеле́вин «Любо́вь к трём цукербри́нам» 2014)

With all his stories, Karaev seems like a clinger who doesn't get that he's not wanted, that he is repulsive and elicits only disgusted shudders. (Pelevin, *Love for Three Zuckerbrins*, 2014)

Пришла́ Ма́шка-пристава́ла. Опя́ть не отвя́жешься от неё до поздна́.

That barnacle, Mashka, came over. I won't be able to get rid of her until late again.

Про́жига

Someone who lives a fast life and wastefully spends money and time on partying and revelry. Typically refers to males. Conveys contempt and strong disapproval.

76   *Entries*

Derived from the verb **прожига́ть** *to burn through* and the noun **прожига́тель** *wastrel*. The expression **прожига́тель жи́зни** *playboy* is synonymous. The adjective **прожжённый** *seasoned* is a related word. **Про́жига** articulates much more negativity than the synonymous **кути́ла**. Semantically close to **гуля́ка** and **пове́са**. Associated with **плут** *rogue*.

See **гуля́ка, кути́ла.**

Днепро́вский счита́лся де́льным тракти́рщиком, но по ви́ду его́ мо́жно бы́ло ду́мать, что он большо́й про́жига и плут. (Н. Варенцо́в «Слы́шанное. Ви́денное. Переду́манное. Пережито́е» 1930–1935)	Dneprovsky was considered a capable innkeeper, but by the look of him, you could say that he was a great wastrel and cheat. (Varentsov, *The Heard. The Seen. The Thought. The Lived*, 1930–1935)
Гуля́ка и про́жига Ми́шка тра́тит де́ньги почём зря, похо́ж на чёрт зна́ет кого́ в свои́ 40.	Mishka, that reveler and rascal wastes money like it's his job. He looks like God knows what at 40.
Я́ростный про́жига он хо́дит по дороги́м рестора́нам, покупа́ет дороги́е ви́на и устра́ивает сумасше́дшие пиру́шки.	A raging partier, he goes to expensive restaurants, buys expensive wines, and throws outrageous parties.

Пройдо́ха

A trickster. A roguish, dishonest cheat. Implies that a person has been around the block. Conveys strong negative emotions.

Жу́лик *cheat*, **моше́нник** *cheat*, and **проны́ра, прощелы́га**, and **ше́льма** are synonymous, though **пройдо́ха** has the connotation of "experienced." Semantically close to **вы́жига, прола́за**. Associated with the adjectives **на́глый** *insolent*, and **хи́трый** *cunning*.

See **вы́жига, прола́за, проны́ра, прощелы́га, ше́льма.**

Он са́мый как есть вы́жига, пройдо́ха, и ро́жа у него́, как у обезья́ны! (И. Турге́нев «Коне́ц Чертопха́нова» 1872)	He's a skinflint, a cheat, and he's got a mug like a monkey! (Turgenev, *Chertopkhanov's End*, 1872)

Я рассказа́ла режиссёру, что э́то должна́ быть тро́гательная де́вочка, а не така́я ста́рая пройдо́ха, как я, и у меня́ есть така́я де́вочка. (Т. Окуне́вская «Татья́нин день» 1998)	I told the director that she should be a touching girl, not an old cheat like me, and that I had just the girl in mind. (Okunevskaya, *Tatyana's Day*, 1998)
Ря́дом на́глый пройдо́ха, прильну́в к це́йсовскому прице́лу, то́же ничего́ не мог разгляде́ть. (И. Бояшо́в «Танки́ст или «Бе́лый тигр» 2008)	The nearby insolent trickster looked into the Zeiss scope, but couldn't see anything either. (Boyashov, *The Tank Operator, or the White Tiger*, 2008)
Сосе́дка на́ша, жу́ткая пройдо́ха – всю́ду суёт свой нос и наду́ть всех норови́т.	Our neighbor is a terrible cheat – sticks her nose everywhere and tries to trick everyone.

Пролаза

Someone who always finds a way to fit in. An opportunist.

Derived from the verb **проле́зть** *to climb through*. The same as **проны́ра** and semantically close to **пройдо́ха** and **прощелы́га**. The nouns **деля́га, карьери́ст** *careerist*, and **конъюнкту́рщик** *opportunist* are associated with **пролаза**.

See **деля́га, пройдо́ха, проны́ра, прощелы́га**.

Но како́в, одна́ко, пролаза, – приба́вил он, – на два дня прие́хал в Москву́, успе́л уже́ съе́здить к генера́л-губерна́тору и получи́ть от него́ приглаше́ние на бал. (А. Пи́семский «Лю́ди сороковы́х годо́в» 1869)	"Still, though, he's such a weasel," he added. "He came to Moscow for two days, and he's already managed to visit the governor general and get an invite to the ball." (Pisemsky, *People of the Forties*, 1869)
Го́льдмана осуди́ли как пролазу, себялю́бца и эго́иста. (С. Ю́рский «Черно́в» 1972–1978)	Goldman was condemned as a weasel and a self-indulgent egotist. (Yursky, *Chernov*, 1972–1978)

Тем не ме́нее он был настоя́щий ру́сский писа́тель, а не деля́га, не карьери́ст, не прола́за, не конъюнкту́рщик. (Ю. Наги́бин «Дневни́к» 1984)	Regardless, he was a real Russian writer, and not a hustler, a careerist, a weasel, an opportunist. (Nagibin, *The Diary*, 1984)

Проны́ра

The same as **прола́за**. A weasel. Articulates disdain and contempt.

Derived from the adjective **проны́рливый** *sneaky, crafty*. Associated with the verbs **проле́зть** *to climb through*, **зале́зть** *to climb in*. Synonymous with **ловка́ч** *trickster*, but conveys more negativity. Semantically close to **пройдо́ха** and **прощелы́га**.

See **прола́за, пройдо́ха, прощелы́га**.

Да по́мнишь, у Васи́лия Васи́льевича домоправи́тельница была́, все его́ причу́ды до то́нкости зна́ла. Всем до́мом верте́ла, проны́ра ба́ба. (С. Григо́рьев «Алекса́ндр Суво́ров» 1939)	Remember, Vasily Vasilievich had a housekeeper who knew all of his whims and subtleties. She ran the whole house, that weasel of a broad. (Grigoryev, *Alexander Suvorov*, 1939)
Понима́л, что э́тот проны́ра иска́л полити́ческие ще́ли, что́бы прони́кнуть наве́рх – к пе́рвому лицу́. (А. Я́ковлев «О́мут па́мяти» 2001)	I understood that that weasel was looking for political holes through which he could sneak upwards to the man in charge. (Yakovlev, *The Slough of Memory*, 2001)
Я про́сто не мог ви́деть, как э́тот проны́ра день за днём обустра́ивает свои́ дели́шки за наш счёт. (М. Петрося́н «Дом, в кото́ром . . .» 2009)	I just couldn't see how that weasel managed to take care of his own issues on our dime day after day. (Petrosyan, *The House Where . . .*, 2009)
Проны́ра Петро́вич все ды́ры зна́ет – уже́ проле́з в комите́т и внёс свою́ ле́пту.	Petrovich, that weasel, knows all the holes – he's already gotten onto the committee and brought his ideas to the table.

Entries 79

Пропо́йца

The same as **пья́ница**. Conveys disapproval and contempt. More frequently refers to males.

Derived from the verb **пропи́ть** *to guzzle*. Does not evoke sympathy, unlike the synonymous **пьянчу́га**. The adjectives **го́рький** *bitter*, **бу́йный** *rowdy*, **зако́нченный** *complete* are used in phrases with the noun.

See **пья́ница**, **пьянчу́га**.

А пото́м уж показа́лось, что он в лу́же гря́зной, как пропо́йца, лежи́т, и от тепла́ сде́лался си́зым, а мунди́р совсе́м скли́зким. (О. Па́влов «Казённая ска́зка» 1993)

Afterwards, it seemed like he was facedown in a dirty puddle, like a drunkard, the warmth turning him blue-grey and his uniform slimy. (Pavlov, *Captain of the Steppe*, 1993)

О том, что папа́ня, бу́йный пропо́йца, почти́ не выхо́дит из тюрьмы́. . . Булдако́в, разуме́ется, сообща́ть воздержа́лся. . . (В. Аста́фьев «Про́кляты и уби́ты» 1995)

Naturally, Buldakov refrained from telling how his daddy was a rowdy boozer who rarely left prison . . . (Astafyev, *Damned and Killed*, 1995)

Меня́ растолка́л кто-то, как оказа́лось, нача́льник корабля́, оди́н глаз се́рый, друго́й ка́рий, пропо́йца и уби́йца. . . (М. Ши́шкин «Вене́рин во́лос» // «Зна́мя» 2005)

As I learned, I was pushed aside by the ship captain, one eye grey, the other brown, a drunkard and a killer. (Shishkin, "Venus's Hair," 2005)

Э́тот гну́сный пропо́йца всю жизнь ей искале́чил.

That wretched drunk ruined her whole life.

Простофи́ля

A simpleton. A simpleminded, slow-witted person who is easy to cheat. Conveys contempt and disrespect, but can also evoke sympathy.

Derived from the adjective **просто́й** *simple*. Associated with the noun **рази́ня**, **дурачи́на** *fool*.

See **рази́ня**.

80　*Entries*

Они́-то пра́вы из суда́ вы́шли, а я, простофи́ля, в ду́рах оста́лась. (М. Салтыко́в-Щедри́н «Пёстрые пи́сьма» 1884)	They walked out of the court in the right, while I, a simpleton, had been made a fool of. (Saltykov-Shchedrin, *Colorful Letters*, 1884)
. . . почему́ он не сообрази́л таку́ю очеви́дную вещь? Простофи́ля. (Д. Гра́нин «Иска́тели» 1954)	. . . why didn't he realize such an obvious thing? Simpleton. (Granin, *The Searchers*, 1954)
Снача́ла, когда́ ста́рший лейтена́нт Тито́в был ещё замести́телем команди́ра по воспита́тельной рабо́те, а про́ще говоря́ – замполи́том, я приняла́ его́ за простофи́лю, кото́рый что ви́дит, то и говори́т. (В. Сини́цына «Му́за и генера́л» 2002)	At first, when senior lieutenant Titov was still second-in-command of character building, or put more simply, the political officer, I took him for a simpleton who sees only what's in front of him. (Sinitsyna, *The Muse and General*, 2002)
Что де́лать с э́тим простофи́лей? Опя́ть надури́ли – оста́лся без гроша́.	What to do with this simpleton? They took advantage of him again, leaving him without a penny.

Прощелы́га

The same as **пройдо́ха**. Conveys disdain and scorn.

Sounds even more negative than the synonymous **моше́нник** *cheat*, **жу́лик** *cheat*, **прохво́ст**, and **афери́ст** *swindler*. Associated with the adjective **наха́льный** *insolent*.

See **пройдо́ха**, **прола́за**, **проны́ра**.

А ма́менька его́ така́я прощелы́га, про́сто че́рез все ме́дные тру́бы прошла́. (Ф. Достое́вский «Село́ Степа́нчиково и его́ обита́тели» 1859)	But his mommy was such a swindler; she went through the whole wringer. (Dostoevsky, *The Village of Stepanchikovo*, 1859)

Entries 81

Это был ужа́снейший
тип, пря́мо прощелы́га,
наха́льный, зано́счивый. . .
(С. М. Волко́нский «Мой
воспомина́ния» 1923–1924)

He was a horrid fellow, a
swindler, insolent and haughty.
(Volkonsky, *My Memories,*
1923–1924)

Он да́же не банди́т. Он пусто́е
ме́сто, жа́лкий прощелы́га.
Всю жизнь оку́чивается во́зле
де́нежных баб. (А. Саве́льев
«Арка́н для букме́кера» 2000)

He's not even a bandit. He's an
empty space, a pitiful scoundrel.
He's spent his whole life sidling
up to rich broads. (Savelyev, *A
Lasso for the Bookmaker,* 2000)

Не обраща́й внима́ния на
э́того афери́ста-прощелы́гу –
всех доста́л, всё выню́хивает,
высма́тривает.

Don't pay attention to that
swindler – everyone's sick of
him, he weasels out every little
thing.

Пустоме́ля

Someone who talks a lot, meaninglessly, and senselessly. Often
refers to a man. Conveys disapproval and disdain.

Derived from the noun **пустосло́в**, literally **пусты́е слова́** *empty
words*. Semantically close to **балабо́лка**. Synonymous with
пустозво́н *windbag*.

See **балабо́лка**.

Ва́ля была́ побойче́й,
поостре́й на язы́к, немно́жко
пустоме́ля. (В. Шукши́н
«Хаха́ль» 1969)

Valya had a brisk and sharp
tongue, she was a bit of a
chatterbox. (Shukshin, *The
Beau,* 1969)

Вы́сечь, отпра́вить в дере́вню,
запере́ть, всё врёт, наврала́
с три ко́роба, лгу́нья,
пустоме́ля . . . (Б. Окуджа́ва
«Путеше́ствие дилета́нтов»
1971–1977)

Stamp her out, send her away
to the country, lock her away,
she tells nothing but lies, the
liar, the blabbermouth . . .
(Okudzhava, *The Dilettantes'
Adventure,* 1971–1977)

Отчего́ я и дура́к, и де́мон, и
пустоме́ля ра́зом? (В. Ерофе́ев

Why am I a fool and a fiend and
a windbag all at the same time?

82   *Entries*

«Москва́-Петушки́» 1973)

От э́того пустоме́ли ни одного́
толко́го сло́ва не добьёшься.

(Yerofeev, *Moscow-Petushki,*
1973)

You can't get a single meaningful
word out of that windbag.

Пья́ница

A drunkard. Someone who abuses alcohol. Stylistically neutral – it
is used merely a statement of fact.

Derived from the adjective **пья́ный** *drunk*. The synonymous
пьянчу́га and **пропо́йца** convey disapproval. The adjectives
беспробу́дный *heavy*, **го́рький** *bitter*, **жа́лкий** *pitiful*, and
запо́йный *unrestrained* are combined with **пья́ница**.

See **пьянчу́га, пропо́йца.**

У па́рня три рога́тки, капка́н
и ма́ма-пья́ница, кото́рая
одобря́ет поведе́ние сы́на и
охо́тно ва́рит суп из голубе́й,
а то и из соба́к, так как в
до́ме не́чего есть, она́ всё
пропива́ет. (Л. Петруше́вская
«Ма́ленькая волше́бница» //
«Октя́брь» 1996)

The guy has three slingshots, a
snare, and a drunkard mother
who approves of her son's
behavior and eagerly makes
soup out of pigeons, or even
dogs, since there's nothing to
eat at home, as she drinks away
every dime. (Petrushevskaya,
"The Little Enchantress," 1996)

Он пья́ница, все его́ угоща́ют,
бе́дного, и он шата́ется
ка́ждый день. (Ю. Три́фонов
«Предвари́тельные ито́ги»
1970)

He's a drunk. Everyone
treats the poor guy, so he
bumbles around day in, day
out. (Trifonov, *Preliminary
Conclusions,* 1970)

Вы́шла за́муж за пья́ницу
неисправи́мого – тепе́рь не
зна́ет, куда́ де́ться от него́.

She married an incorrigible
drunk and now doesn't know
how to get away.

Пьянчу́га (пьянчу́жка)

The same as **пья́ница**. Conveys disapproval, but can also evoke
sympathy.

Entries　83

Derived from the adjective **пья́ный** *drunk*. The dimunitive **пьянчу́жка** articulates pity, but even more disrespect. The synonymous **пропо́йца** does not evoke sympathy.

See **пья́ница**, **пропо́йца**.

Попроша́йка-пьянчу́жка был челове́к совсе́м скве́рный, бу́йный и льсти́вый, и по всему́ бы́ло ви́дно, что он как-нибудь там обольсти́л Семёна Ива́новича. (Ф. Достое́вский «Господи́н Проха́рчин» 1846)

The drunkard beggar was a hateful, rowdy, and adulatory individual, and everyone could see how he sweet-talked Semyon Ivanovich. (Dostoevsky, *Mister Prokharchin*, 1846)

Како́й-то пьянчу́га броди́л вдоль о́череди и скрипе́л зуба́ми, сло́вно кали́тка на ветру́. (В. Аксёнов «Апельси́ны из Маро́кко» 1962)

Some drunk was wandering up and down the line, gnashing his teeth, sounding as if he were a gate creaking in the wind. (Aksyonov, *Oranges from Morocco*, 1962)

Ка́ждый день я ви́жу в окно́ одну́ и ту же пьянчу́жку, оде́тую в неизме́нные спорти́вные штаны́ и вя́заную ша́почку, с пла́стиковым паке́том, в кото́рый она́ собира́ет буты́лки. (А. Бра́во «Коменда́нтский час для ла́сточек» // «Сиби́рские огни́» 2012)

Every day, I see out the window the same drunk, wearing the same sweat pants and knitted hat, with a plastic bag that she used to collect bottles. (Bravo, "A Curfew for Swallows," 2012)

Ани́сим – ничто́жество, ленты́й и пьянчу́га, и ничто́ его́ уже́ не спасёт.

Anisim is a mediocre, lazy drunk, and nothing can help him now.

Работя́га[1]

A hard worker. Expresses positive emotions and approval.

Derived from the verb **рабо́тать** *to work* and the noun **рабо́та** *work*.

Ну а вторы́м челове́ком ста́ла моя́ мать, работя́га, вла́стная, хозя́йственная, аккура́тная; навяза́в де́душке свою́ семью́, она́ счита́ла себя́ обя́занной рабо́тать за двои́х . . . (А. Рыбако́в «Тяжёлый песо́к» 1978)

My mother became the second person – a hard worker, imperious, assiduous, tidy; having saddled grandpa with her family, she saw it as her duty to work hard enough for two . . . (Rybakov, *Heavy Sand*, 1978)

Он настоя́щий журнали́ст, общи́тельный, с кре́пкой хва́ткой и безоши́бочными вопро́сами, работя́га. . . (Д. Гра́нин «Ме́сяц вверх нога́ми» 1966)

He's a real journalist, sociable, with a firm grasp on things and probing questions, a hard worker . . . (Granin, *The Overturned Crescent*, 1966)

А тепе́рь отстро́ился, завёл хозя́йство, кре́пкое, потому́ что сам работя́га. (А. Приста́вкин «Ваго́нчик мой да́льний» 2005)

But he's built back up, he has a household now, a strong one, seeing as he's a hard worker himself. (Pristavkin, *My Faraway Little Carriage*, 2005)

Валенти́на была́ работя́гой и без де́ла сиде́ть не уме́ла – должна́ была́ что-то де́лать то ли в саду́, то ли по хозя́йству.

Valentina was a hard worker and didn't know how to sit around doing nothing. She always had to be doing something out in the garden or in her house.

Работя́га²

A worker without formal qualifications, as opposed to someone with a higher education. Typically refers to males. Neutral or articulates a positive overtone.

Derived from the verb **рабо́тать** *to work* and the noun **рабо́та** *work*. The phrase **просто́й работя́га**, literally *simple worker* is often used in discourse.

В э́тот моме́нт в камо́рку вахтёра загляну́л како́й-то работя́га в ва́тнике.

At that moment, some worker in a cotton coat looked into the watchman's cubicle. (Tronina,

Entries 85

(Т. Тро́нина «Никогда́ не говори́ «навсегда́» 2004)

Never Say "Forever," 2004)

Дире́ктор заво́да обосно́ванно сомнева́ется в и́скренности нача́льника це́ха, тот в свою́ о́чередь работя́ге доверя́ет бо́льше, чем ма́стеру. (А. Азо́льский «Диверса́нт» // «Но́вый мир» 2002)

The plant director reasonably doubts the sincerity of the foreman, who, in turn, trusts the drudge more than the master. (Azol'sky, "The Commando," 2002)

Дя́дя Жо́ра говори́л, что то́лько несмышлёный болва́н мо́жет нали́ть спи́рту работя́ге, не зако́нчившему рабо́ту. (Д. Кара́лис «Космона́вт» // «Нева́» 2002)

Uncle Zhora said that only an unsophisticated moron could give booze to a worker who hasn't finished working yet. (Karalis, "The Cosmonaut," 2002)

Никола́й Семёнович – работя́га, хотя́ квалифика́ции хвата́ет на двои́х.

Nikolai Semyonovich is just a line worker, though he's qualified enough for two.

Раззя́ва

Someone who overlooks or misses important things. Expresses strong disapproval and criticism.

Associated with the verbs **недосмотре́ть** *to overlook,* **упусти́ть** *to miss,* **пропусти́ть** *to miss,* and **прозева́ть** *to miss.* Synonymous with **рази́ня**. Semantically close to **зева́ка** and **растя́па**.

See **зева́ка, рази́ня, растя́па**.

Что же ты, раззя́ва, за свои́м ребёнком не смо́тришь! (Т. Крю́кова «Стра́жи поря́дка» // «Нау́ка и жизнь» 2008)

You scatterbrain, why aren't you looking after your kid! (Kryukova, "Guards of Order," 2008)

Я на́чал удо́бней устра́иваться за кусто́м, гля́нул – нет поплавка́: «Раззя́ва!» (В. Аста́фьев «Царь-ры́ба» 1974)

I started getting more comfortably situated in my bush. I glanced out at the water – the float was gone. "You scatterbrain!" (Astafyev, *The Fish King,* 1974)

86 *Entries*

Эх ты, разя́ва! Неуже́ли ни одно́й лепёшки не успе́л сля́мзить?! (Г. Бе́лых, А. Пантеле́ев «Респу́блика ШКИД» 1926)

You scatterbrain! Did you really fail to make a single pancake?! (Belykh, Panteleev, *The Republic of ShKID*, 1926)

Ну и разя́ва – опя́ть серёжки потеря́ла?

What a scatterbrain – did you lose your earrings again?

Рази́ня

A scatterbrain. An inattentive person who fails to notice things or misses important things. Used when the speaker wishes to criticize someone.

Associated with the phrase **рази́нуть рот** meaning *not to pay attention*. Synonymous with **разя́ва**. Semantically close to **зева́ка** and **растя́па**.

See **зева́ка, разя́ва, растя́па**.

Встава́й, рази́ня, мы уже́ до А́фрики долете́ли, а ты всё дры́хнешь. (В. По́стников «Каранда́ш и Самоде́лкин в стране́ людое́дов» 1996)

Get up, scatterbrain, we're already in Africa, and you're still lolling about. (Postnikov, *Pencil and Handyman in the Land of Maneaters,* 1996)

Соболе́й нигде́ не ви́дно. Прозева́л! Рази́ня! Размазня́! Недотёпа! (Г. Алексе́ев «Зелёные берега́» 1983–1984)

There are no sables to be seen anywhere. I missed them! Scatterbrain! Ninny! Stupid oaf! (Alekseev, *Green Shores,* 1983–1984)

Во́йско, разуме́ется, потащи́лось за ним, и оди́н из гре́ков, рази́ня, потеря́л золоту́ю моне́ту. (С. Благо́в «Улы́бка Анахи́ты» // «Ю́ность» 1971)

Naturally, the troop started after him, and one of the more scatterbrained of the Greeks lost a gold coin. (Blagov, *Anahit's Smile,* 1971)

Ох э́тот рази́ня – всё теря́ет, ничего́ в ру́ки дать нельзя́.

Oh, that scatterbrain – he loses everything, you can't give him anything.

Entries 87

Размазня́

An undetermined person, someone who does not have strength of character, who cannot stand up for him or herself. Conveys contempt, disdain, and disrespect.

Ма́мля and **ню́ня** can be synonymous. Its synonym **ро́хля** additionally implies physical frailty.

See **ма́мля, ню́ня, ро́хля.**

Вста́ла с утра́ зла́я на себя́, на то, что вчера́ так распусти́ла ню́ни. Размазня́! (М. Ши́шкин «Вене́рин во́лос» // «Зна́мя» 2005)	I got up in the morning mad at myself for crying like a baby yesterday. Ninny! (Shishkin, *Venus's Hair*, 2005)
. . . не тот ли э́то размазня́, что без бо́я отда́л врагу́ зна́тный трофе́й? (В. Аста́фьев «За́теси» // «Но́вый мир» 1999)	. . . isn't that the wuss who gave up a prized trophy to his foe without a fight? (Astafyev, *Notches*, 1999)
Не поня́тно, как тако́й размазня́ дослужи́лся до нача́льника отде́ла.	It's unclear how such a ninny got to be the division head.
Го́споди, счита́ли тебя́ за си́льного челове́ка, а ты оказа́лся размазнёй.	God, we thought you were a strong person, but it turns out you're a wimp.

Растя́па

A clumsy individual who does everything poorly and thoughtlessly. Conveys reproach, but may also be said remorsefully.

Semantically close to **разза́ва, рази́ня,** and **растеря́ха.**

See **разза́ва, рази́ня, растеря́ха.**

И что ока́зывается: э́то ло́жная трево́га! Растя́па како́й-то дал по оши́бке.	And then it turns out it was a false alarm! Some klutz gave it by accident. (Gorlanova,

88   *Entries*

(Н. Горланова «Что-то
хорошее» 1987–1999)

Something Good, 1987–1999)

К концу фильма они
умыкают невесту от
жениха-растяпы. (Л. Гурченко
«Аплодисменты» 1994–2003)

By the end of the film, they
steal the bride away from
the shlemiel of a groom.
(Gurchenko, *Applause,*
1994–2003)

Это рабочий вставлял
стекло в окно, да так и
забыл стремянку, растяпа.
(Д. Рубина «Медная
шкатулка» 2015)

It was the ditzy worker that put
the glass into the window and
left the ladder there. (Rubina,
The Copper Box, 2015)

Ну и растяпа же у нас выросла.
Что ни попроси, ничего
сделать нормально не может.

Our child grew up to be such
a klutz. Can't do anything
properly.

Растеряха

Someone who constantly loses things. Conveys disapproval.

Derived from the verb **терять** *to lose.* Semantically close to
раззява and растяпа.

See **раззява, растяпа.**

Вещи его береги́те, а
то он у меня растеряха.
(К. Станюкович «Вокруг
света на Коршуне» 1895)

Take his things, or else he'll
lose them, my little woolhead.
(Stanyukovich, *Around the
World on a Vulture,* 1895)

А Митрий кричит: «Растеряха
ты! Я думал, у тебя капитал
скоплен, а разве у растерях
капитал бывает». (Н. Тэффи
«Брошечка» 1911)

Meanwhile, Mitry yelled:
"You woolhead! I thought you
had assets to speak of, but
woolheads don't have assets."
(Teffi, *The Little Brooch,* 1911)

Наша растеряха пришла без
шарфика и перчаток – опять
потеряла или забыла где-то.

Our little woolhead came
home without her scarf
and gloves – she lost them
somewhere again.

Entries 89

Растрёпа

A careless individual with a sloppy, careless appearance. Creates the impression that one does not take care of him or herself properly. Conveys disapproval.

Derived from the verb **растрепа́ться** *to ruffle one's hair*. Synonymous with **неря́ха**, although the latter typically refers to someone untidy. **Аккура́тный челове́к** *tidy individual* is antonymous.

See **неря́ха**.

Ири́на сбро́сила плато́к с головы́, посмотре́лась в зе́ркало: «Фу, растрёпа. . . » Опра́вила во́лосы, отошла́ к комо́ду у да́льней стены́. (С. Мстисла́вский «Грач – пти́ца весе́нняя» 1937)	Irina threw the scarf off her head, peered into the mirror: "Ugh, you mophead . . ." She fixed her hair and went to the dresser at the far wall. (Mstislavsky, *A Rook Is a Springtime Bird*, 1937)
Маркс – он и в жи́зни был поря́дочный растрёпа, ему́ не́когда бы́ло следи́ть за собо́й, потому́ что мы́слям его́ бы́ло те́сно в любо́й благоприли́чной оболо́чке. (М. Эпште́йн «Ле́нин-Ста́лин» // «Родни́к» 1989)	Marx was a scrupulous mophead in life, he never had time to take care of himself, as his ideas would feel cramped in any pretty-looking wrapper. (Epstein, "Lenin-Stalin," 1989)
Я же была́ неря́ха и растрёпа – не бо́лее, впро́чем, чем вся́кая де́вочка, с шести́ лет погружённая в кни́ги и лет до четы́рнадцати вообще́ не посмотре́вшая на себя́ в зе́ркало. (Р. Фру́мкина «О нас – наискосо́к» 1995)	I was a ragbag and a mophead – no different from any girl who had been buried in books from six until she was fourteen and never had time to look in the mirror. (Frumkina, *A Slanted Look at Us,* 1995)
Что ж ты тако́й растрёпа? Нау́чишься причёсываться ко́гда-нибудь?	Why are you such a mophead? Will you ever learn how to use a comb?

Рёва

Someone who cries often. Frequently refers to children. Conveys disapproval and disdain.

Derived from the verb **реветь** *to bawl*. The dimunitive **рёвушка** expresses fondness. Its synonym **нюня** additionally indicates someone who whines and moans a lot, while the synonym **плакса** expresses less negativity. The phrase **рёва-корова** *crybaby* is used when children tease one another.

See **нюня, плакса**.

Как он ни старался удержаться, слёзы всё-таки же покатились из его глаз, и он, закрыв лицо руками, прижался к печке. – Эх ты, рёва-корова! – произнёс Грузов презрительно . . . (А. Куприн «На переломе» 1900)

Try as he could, he couldn't keep the tears from rolling down his cheeks. Hiding his face behind his hands, he pressed up against the stove. "You crybaby!" said Gruzov scornfully. (Kuprin, *At the Breaking Point*, 1900)

Давно она уже не маленькая и совсем не рёва, как раньше.

She hasn't been a little girl for a long time, and she's not a crybaby anymore.

Чуть что он плачет – остановить нельзя. Такая рёва – ужас просто.

He starts crying at the slightest provocation, and it's impossible to make him stop. He's such a crybaby, it's awful.

Ровня

An individual who is someone else's equal socially, financially, intellectually, or in some other way. Stylistically neutral. Mainly used in contemporary Russian in the nominative case.

Derived from the adjective **ровный** *even*. Antonymous with **неровня**, which is used more frequently in contemporary Russian.

See **неровня**.

Потому́ что не то́лько был им ро́вня, а мог счита́ться и украше́нием – сперва́ компа́нии, тепе́рь клу́ба. (А. На́йман «Все и ка́ждый» // «Октя́брь» 2003)

Because he wasn't just their peer – he could be considered a decoration, the company's first, and now the club's. (Nayman, "Each and Every One," 2003)

А вот дочь у них – подро́сток, нам ро́вня, бе́ленькая, голена́стая и, как вы́яснилось, смешли́вая. (А. Приста́вкин «Ваго́нчик мой да́льний» 2005)

But their daughter's a teen, our peer, fair-skinned, long-legged, and, as it turned out, easily amused. (Pristavkin, *My Faraway Little Carriage*, 2005)

Я́сно же, что те, что из джи́па, не наёмный персона́л, а цы́почка с бога́тым па́пиком, зна́чит, вопро́сы им мо́жет задава́ть то́лько ро́вня. (М. Зоси́мкина «Ты проснёшься» 2015)

It was clear that the girl from the jeep wasn't an employee, but a chicklet with a rich daddy, which meant that only an equal could ask her questions. (Zosimkina, *You Will Wake Up*, 2015)

Ро́хля

A frail individual who is undetermined, hesitating, and unenergetic. Conveys contempt, disdain, and disrespect.

This noun is associated with the adjective **ры́хлый** *frail, crumbly*. The synonyms **мя́мля** and **размазня́** emphasize moral rather than physical virtues.

See **мя́мля, размазня́**.

С его ро́стом, ба́сом и э́такой нару́жной, молодцева́той незави́симостью он ещё како́й-то паца́н и ро́хля. (Ю. Три́фонов «Предвари́тельные ито́ги» 1970)

Despite his height, bass, and dashing swagger, he is still a kid and a chump. (Trifonov, *Preliminary Conclusions*, 1970)

– Ваш дежу́рный – ро́хля, он три дня батаре́ю иска́ть

Your security guard is a chump, he'll spend three days looking

92 Entries

бу́дет. (Б. Васи́льев «Бы́ли и
небы́ли» 1988)

for that battery. (Vasiliev, *True
Stories and Malarkey*, 1988)

Кака́я же ты, Со́ня, ро́хля,
обвести́ тебя́ вокру́г па́льца
ничего́ не сто́ит.

You're such a chump, Sonya,
it's so easy to pull the wool
over your eyes.

С э́тим ро́хлей никто́ де́ла
име́ть не хо́чет и не бу́дет.

Nobody wants anything to do
with that chump, and they won't.

Самоу́чка

Someone who studied by oneself, without supervision. Used in many
cases as an appositive clarifying another, typically masculine, noun,
e.g. **инжене́р-самоу́чка** *self-taught engineer*, **меха́ник-самоу́чка**
self-taught mechanical engineer. In general, it more frequently
refers to males. Stylistically neutral.

Derived from the words **сам у́чится** *to study by oneself*. The phrase
остря́к-самоу́чка *smartass* is used rather often in discourse.

Ха́им был для своего́
вре́мени – и для на́шего
городка́ – челове́ком
дово́льно образо́ванным,
хотя́ и самоу́чка. (А. Рыбако́в
«Тяжёлый песо́к» 1978)

For his own time – and for our
village – Chaim was a fairly
educated man, even though
he was self-taught. (Rybakov,
Heavy Sand, 1978)

Помолчи́, остря́к-самоу́чка, –
предви́дя но́вую волну́
ёрничания, проговори́л
Гу́ров. (Н. Лео́нов «Лека́рство
от жи́зни» 2001)

"Be quiet, you smartass," said
Gurov, heading off the wave of
wisecracks. (Leonov, *Medicine
From Life*, 2001)

Евстигне́я – как скрипи́чного
самоу́чку – упекли́ во
вторы́е скри́пки. (Б. Евсе́ев
«Евстигне́й» // «Октя́брь» 2010)

Yevstigney was assigned to
be in the second strings, as
he was a self-taught violinist.
(Yevseyev, "Yevstigney," 2010)

Ба́бушка была́ о́чень
образо́ванной, и никто́ не
дога́дывался, что была́ она́
самоу́чкой.

Grandma was very educated,
and no one ever suspected that
she was self-taught.

Entries 93

Свято́ша

In contemporary language, denotes a hypocrite or someone who pretends that he/she is very pious or prude. Conveys disdain and condemnation.

Derived from the adjective **свято́й** *holy* and the noun **свя́тость** *holiness*. Semantically close to **лицеме́р** *hypocrite*, which stresses someone's general hypocritical behavior, while the synonymous **ханжа́** stresses one's hypocritical attitude towards sex.

See **ханжа́**.

Все у неё вру́ньи, одна́ она́ то́лько свято́ша! (Л. Ча́рская «Прию́тки» 1907)	To hear her say it, everyone's a liar, she alone is pure! (Charskaya, *Little Havens*, 1907)
Но вы же мне говори́ли, что Фузи́нти – свято́ша, бре́згует да́же прикаса́ться к же́нщинам? (А. Амфитеа́тров «Ма́рья Лу́сьева за грани́цей» 1911)	But you told me that Fuzinti is a puritan hypocrite, that he shrinks even from touching women. (Amfiteatrov, *Maria Lusyeva Abroad*, 1911)
Кручи́нин во́все не свято́ша, он не страда́ет ма́нией пури́зма – сво́йством лицеме́ров. (Н. Шпано́в «Учени́к чароде́я» 1956)	Kruchinin isn't a holier-than-though hypocrite – he doesn't suffer from delusions of purism, which hypocrites have. (Shpanov, *The Sorcerer's Apprentice*, 1956)
Уж ко́ли э́та свято́ша обха́живает его́, так мне сам бог веле́л. (Ф. Абра́мов «Бра́тья и сёстры» 1958)	If *this* hypocrite is looking after him, then I can too, no problem. (Abramov, *Brothers and Sisters*, 1958)

Симпатя́га

Refers to someone nice, typically a man. Evokes positive feelings, chiefly fondness. Informal and expresses familiarity.

Derived from the adjective **симпати́чный** *cute* which is a more neutral. Synonymous with **миля́га**.

See **миля́га**.

Бахта́мов – халту́рщик и не
бог весть что, но симпатя́га и
весёлый челове́к. (Г. Эфрон
«Дневники́» 1941–1943)

Bakhtamov bungles everything
he does, but he's very much a
cutie and a joyful one at that.
(Efron, *Diaries*, 1941–1943)

Скоре́е всего́ ей нра́вился
не́кий студе́нт из на́шей
компа́нии, краса́вец и
симпатя́га с а́лым ро́тиком,
лучи́стыми глаза́ми. . .
(В. Ката́ев «Ю́ношеский
рома́н» 1982)

Most likely, she had a crush on
a student from our company,
a handsome and likeable
fellow with scarlet lips and
shining eyes . . . (Katayev, *An
Adolescent Love Story*, 1982)

Добре́йший мужи́к,
симпатя́га, Шау́ль, то́лько
глупова́т, верне́е, о́чень
наи́вен. . . (Д. Ру́бина
«Ру́сская канаре́йка. Блу́дный
сын» 2014)

Shaul' is a kind-hearted man,
a cutie, only he's somewhat
foolish, or rather very naïve . . .
(Rubina, *Russian Canary. The
Prodigal Son*, 2014)

Сквалы́га

A penny-pincher. A miserly and stingy individual. Expresses an
extremely strong negative overtone. Scornful.

Derived from the verb **сквалы́жничать** *to be stingy*. Synonymous with **скря́га**, **скупердя́й** *tightwad*, and **жмот** *cheapskate*.
Semantically close to **жа́дина**, which focusses on one's unwilling-
ness to share something and can be used to address children, unlike
сквалы́га.

See **жа́дина**, **скря́га**.

То́лько тётка оста́лась,
сквалы́га: ко́мнату в Москве́
име́ла, а племя́нницу вот
родну́ю не пусти́ла к себе́.
(Н. Коже́вникова «Шу́ра и
На́стенька» 1988)

Only my penny-pinching aunt
is left: she had an apartment in
Moscow, but she didn't even
let her own niece stay with her.
(Kozhevnikova, *Shura and
Nasten'ka*, 1988)

Пожале́л до́брых сапо́г,
ста́рый сквалы́га, –

"He took pity on the good
boots," whined Zhikhar . . .

пожа́ловался Жиха́рь. . .
(М. Успе́нский «Там, где нас
нет» 1995)

(Uspensky, *Where We Aren't*,
1995)

Му́драя немолода́я сквалы́га
Со́фья Вла́сьевна то́чно
рассчита́ла, что, зако́нно
вы́ехав за рубе́ж, Йрочка
суме́ет получи́ть огро́мные
де́ньги, накопи́вшиеся на
счету́ опа́льного лауреа́та.
(Н. Вороне́ль «Без прикра́с.
Воспомина́ния» 2003)

The wise, elderly
penny-pincher, Sofya
Vlasyevna, accurately
calculated that after legally
leaving the country, Irochka
would be able to get her hands
on the massive amount of
money that accrued in the fallen
laureate's account. (Voronel',
*Without Embelishments.
Recollections*, 2003)

Э́тот сквалы́га никому́ де́нег
взаймы́ не даст и за копе́йку
уда́вится.

That penny-pincher won't loan
money to anyone and would
throw a fit over a single cent.

Скря́га

A penny-pincher. A miserly and stingy individual. Expresses an
extremely strong negative overtone. Scornful.

Derived from the verb **скря́жничать** *to be tightfisted*. Synonymous with **сквалы́га**, **скупердя́й** *tightwad*, and **жмот** *cheapskate*.
Semantically close to **жа́дина**, which focusses on one's unwilling-
ness to share something and can be used to address children, unlike
скря́га.

See **жа́дина**, **сквалы́га**.

Они́ вы́пили горя́чего
сби́тню – ссыла́ясь на
вое́нные времена́, скря́га
эконо́м вме́сто ча́ю дава́л
им тепе́рь сби́тень, по их
мне́нию, немилосе́рдно
нажива́ясь на э́том.
(Ю. Тыня́нов «Пу́шкин» 1936)

They drank some hot sbiten –
pointing to the fact that there
was a war going on, the
penny-pinching steward gave
them only sbiten, capitalizing
on the situation, as they
thought. (Tynyanov, *Pushkin*,
1936)

Управи́тель был стра́шный скря́га, он копи́л де́ньги, ворова́л у хозя́ина, обсчи́тывал рабо́чих, за гроши́ и́ли спирт скупа́л у бродя́г и стара́телей зо́лото. (В. Шишко́в «Емелья́н Пугачёв: Истори́ческое повествова́ние» 1942)

The manager was a terrible penny-pincher; he stockpiled money, stole from the owners, shortchanged the workers, bought gold from the miners for pennies or booze. (Shishkov, *Yemelyan Pugachev*, 1942)

Муж-скря́га и госте́й стара́ется не звать – ли́шние расхо́ды. (Т. Ивано́ва «Портре́т моего́ му́жа» // «Семе́йный до́ктор» 2002)

My tightfisted husband tries not to have guests over either – needless expenses. (Ivanova, "A Portrait of My Husband," 2002)

Тётушка А́нна была́ жутча́йшая скря́га, и никто́ да́же не пыта́лся от неё что-то получи́ть.

Auntie Anna was a terrible cheapskate, and nobody even tried to get anything from her.

Скромня́га

A very modest individual. Expresses positive emotions, but can also be used negatively to imply that someone only looks modest, but in reality is not. The phrase **на вид скромня́га** *looks shy* can be used in this case.

Derived from the adjective **скро́мный** *modest*. Semantically close to **засте́нчивый** *timid* and **стыдли́вый** *bashful*.

Смотри́ ж ты, на вид скромня́га, а сра́зу берёт быка́ за рога́. (Ю. Наги́бин «Расска́зы о Гага́рине» 1979)

Look at that! Seems shy, but immediately takes the bull by the horns. (Nagibin, *Stories About Gagarin*, 1979)

. . . сего́дня ви́дим како́го-нибудь скромня́гу по телеви́зору, а уже́ че́рез полго́да нам пока́зывают его́

. . . today, we see some shy person on the TV, but half a year later we see his super fancy villas in other

Entries 97

супернаворо́ченные ви́ллы за бугро́м. . . (А. Грачёв «Я́рый про́тив видеопира́тов» 1999)

countries . . . (Grachev, *Fierce Against Video Pirates*, 1999)

Я смире́нницей росла́, он – гордецо́м, Я – «скромня́гой» из хрони́ческих отли́чниц, Он – «стиля́гой» с демони́ческим лицо́м. (Д. Карапетя́н «Влади́мир Высо́цкий. Воспомина́ния» 2002)

I grew up a meek woman, he grew up arrogant. I was one of those modest, chronic A-students, he was a stilyaga with a demonic face. (Karapetyan, *Vladimir Vysotsky. Recollections*, 2002)

Ле́на всегда́ каза́лась скромня́гой – не высо́вывалась, вела́ себя́ ти́хо.

Lena always seemed modest – she never distinguished herself, was always quiet.

Сладкое́жка

Someone who enjoys sweet food.

Synonymous with the noun **сласте́на** and is semantically close to the noun **ла́комка**.

See **ла́комка, сласте́на**.

Вообще́-то она́ не сладкое́жка. Но кля́нчила конфе́ты постоя́нно. (А. Пантеле́ев «На́ша Ма́ша» 1966)

In general, she doesn't have a sweet tooth. But she would always bum candy off people. (Panteleev, *Our Masha*, 1966)

Он был сладкое́жка, люби́л дома́шний ую́т и наслажда́лся им. (В. Коже́вников «Щит и меч» 1968)

He had a sweet tooth, loved the comfort of home, and reveled in it. (Kozhevnikov, *Shield and Sword*, 1968)

Све́та была́ жу́ткой сладкое́жкой, и роди́тели пря́тали от неё конфе́ты.

Sveta had a terrible sweet tooth, and her parents hid all the candy.

Ми́ша был с де́тства сладкое́жкой, и с во́зрастом не переста́л люби́ть сла́дкое.

Misha had always had a sweet tooth, and age did not dull his love of sweets.

Сластёна

Someone who enjoys sweet food.

Synonymous with the noun **сладкоёжка** and semantically close to the noun **ла́комка**.

See **ла́комка, сладкоёжка.**

О́трок и ю́ноша Го́голь – сластёна, лю́бит пло́тно пое́сть; во рту́ у него́ постоя́нно сла́дкое. (А. Воро́нский «Го́голь» 1934)	As an adolescent and a youth, Gogol has a sweet tooth and loves a filling meal: he is constantly eating sweets. (Voronsky, *Gogol'*, 1934)
Он у вас большо́й сластёна, я кладу́ ему́ в стака́н шесть куско́в са́хара. (А. Ла́рина «Незабыва́емое» 1989)	He has a terrible sweet tooth, I put six sugar cubes in his cup. (Larina, *Unforgettable*, 1989)
Дед был ужа́сный сластёна и страда́л от того́, что ему́ нельзя́ бы́ло есть конфе́ты.	Grandpa had an awful sweet tooth and suffered from not being able to eat candy.
У Та́ни, изве́стной сластёны, всегда́ боля́т зу́бы, но она́ всё равно́ поеда́ет сла́дкое в огро́мном коли́честве.	Tanya, with her famous sweet tooth, constantly has a toothache, but she still consumes an enormous amount of sweets.

Со́ня

A dormouse. Someone who likes to sleep a lot and is always sleepy. Articulates condescension. Can sound fond, especially when addressing children.

Derived from the noun **сон** *dream.*

Ну нет, я со́ня, а вот сейча́с спать совсе́м не хо́чется. (С. Жема́йтис «Больша́я лагу́на» 1977)	Well no, I'm a dormouse, but I don't want to sleep at all right now. (Žemaitis, *The Big Laguna*, 1977)
Встава́й, со́ня! Уже́ по́здно – проспи́шь всё со́лнце.	Get up, sleepyhead! It's late, you'll miss the sun.

Ну что ты, Никита, всё
зеваешь? Соня ты эдакий.

Why do you keep yawning,
Nikita? You're such a
sleepyhead.

Стиляга

A young person whose clothes, hairstyle, manners, and taste differ
from what is standard. The **стиляги** (plural) subculture was popular
in the Soviet Union in the late 50s and 60s. Expresses disapproval.
The diminutive **стиляжка** conveys disdain.

Derived from the noun **стиль** *style*. Synonymous with **пижон** *fop*.

И тут подходит к нам девица,
такая, братцы, красавица, такая
стиляга, прямо с картинки.
(В. Аксёнов «Апельсины из
Марокко» 1962)

And then, boys this girl comes up
to us, a beauty, such a stilyaga,
as if from a picture. (Aksyonov,
Oranges from Morocco, 1962)

Видно, приезжий, одет
по-городскому. Какой-нибудь,
понимаешь, будущий
стиляга... (Н. Дубов «Небо с
овчинку» 1966)

He was clearly from out
of town, dressed in city
clothes. Some future stilyaga,
no doubt ... (Dubov, *The
Condensed Sky*, 1966)

Старый стал, башка
плешивая, волосы – всё ж
таки, по моде, длинные,
стилягу не переделаешь –
бахромой висят, борода
клоками, да и серая...
(А. Кабаков «Масло, запятая,
холст» 1987)

He's gotten old, thinning, his
hair still stylishly long – there's
no changing a stilyaga: his hair
still hangs down like drapes,
his beard drooping in tufts, and
grey to boot ... (Kabakov, *Oil,
Comma, Canvas*, 1987)

Какой он был красивый
в этот день, в пёстром
пиджаке и тёмных брюках,
с бархатной бабочкой, такой
весь свободный, раскованный,
очаровательный стиляга!
(Г. Щербакова «Год Алёны»
1996)

He was so pretty that day,
dressed in a patchwork suit and
dark pants, with a velvet bowtie,
a free, untethered, charming
stilyaga! (Shcherbakova,
Alyona's Year, 1996)

100   *Entries*

Сутя́га

A barrator. A person who eagerly pursues litigation. Expresses contempt and disrespect.

Derived from the noun **сутя́жник** *litigant* and the verb **сутя́жничать** *to litigate.*

Есть у нас в комиссариа́те одна́ ста́рая де́ва – то́щая – с ба́нтом – влюблённая в свои́х великово́зрастных бра́тьев-враче́й, достаю́щая им по де́тским ка́рточкам шокола́д, – проны́ра, сутя́га... (М. Цвета́ева «Мои́ слу́жбы» 1919)

There is an old maid in our commissariat – skinny, with a bow in her hair, in love with her overaged fellow physicians, getting them chocolates with children's coupons – a weasel and a barrator ... (Tsvetaeva, *My Service*, 1919)

Он был сутя́га, оста́вивший своему́ сы́ну ни́щую хи́жину, ту́чных жён и бычка́, к кото́рому не́ было па́ры. (И. Ба́бель «Багра́т-Оглы́ и глаза́ его́ быка́» 1927)

He was a barrator who left his son a destitute hut, corpulent wives, and a pitiful bull without a mate. (Babel, *Bagrat-Ogly and the Eyes of His Bull*, 1927)

По́сле сме́рти стару́хи на́чал тя́жбу со свои́м beau-frère'ом из-за до́ма, вообще́ оказа́лся бурбо́ном и сутя́гой. (М. Кузми́н «Дневни́к 1934 го́да» 1934)

After the old woman's death, he brought a suit against his beau-frère for the house and generally turned out to be a churl and a barrator. (Kuzmin, *The Diary from 1934*, 1934)

Доце́нт э́тот был по́длый сутя́га, кото́рый хоте́л подключи́ть к свое́й сугу́бо ли́чной скло́ке центра́льную пре́ссу. (С. Кара́-Мурза́ «Антисове́тский прое́кт» 2002)

The dean was a villainous barrator who wanted to get the press involved in his private squabble. (Kara-Murza, *The Anti-Soviet Project*, 2002)

Тарато́рка

Someone who speaks quickly and a lot. Expresses disapproval.

Entries 101

Derived from **таратóрить** *to chatter*. Synonymous with the figurative meaning of the instrument **трещóтка**, which can be used to mean *chatterbox*. Semantically close to **балабóлка** and **болтýн** *gossiper*.

See **балабóлка**.

Я ужé пя́тый день вмéсте с Мáртой, и я бóльше не могý – головá трещи́т от э́той таратóрки, онá не умéет находи́ться в тишинé.	I've been with Marta for five days, and I can't take it anymore – my head is splitting apart, that chatterbox is incapable of existing in silence.
Ты таратóрка и трещóтка. Мóжешь не тарахтéть, а говори́ть мéдленнее и вня́тно?	You're a chatterbox. Could you stop babbling and speak more slowly and clearly?
Ну зачасти́ла таратóрка – ничегó не поня́тно. Вот так всегдá – таратóрит вмéсто тогó, чтóбы тóлком объясни́ть.	The chatterbox went off again – couldn't understand a thing she was saying. Same as always – she jabbers on instead of giving a proper explanation.

Тёзка

A namesake. Somebody who has the same name as someone else. Stylistically neutral.

Онá былá вáша тёзка и соотéчественница. (Ю. Домбрóвский «Факультéт ненýжных вещéй» 1978)	She was your namesake and your compatriot. (Dombrovsky, *The Department of Unnecessary Things*, 1978)
Мой тёзка, влюблённый в Зинаи́ду, он же сын счастли́вого любóвника, он же глáвный герóй – ины́ми словáми, я? (В. Белоýсова «Вторóй вы́стрел» 2000)	My namesake, in love with Zinaida, the son of a fortunate lover, the main protagonist – in other words, me? (Belousova, *The Second Shot*, 2000)
Станислáвский, как егó тёзка Кóстя Трéплев из чéховской «Чáйки», снóва	Stanislavsky, like his namesake from *The Seagull*, Kostya Treplev, once again began

стал иска́ть но́вых форм. . . (М. Шима́дина «Игра́ по прави́лам и без» // «Экспе́рт» 2013).	to search for new forms . . . (Shimadina, "A Fair and Unfair Game," 2013)
А восходя́щая звезда́ сбо́рной, по́лный тёзка и внук легенда́рного тре́нера Ви́ктор Ти́хонов офо́рмил дубль. (А. Беля́ев «Спорт. Стадио́н» // «Огонёк» 2014)	But the team's rising star, the namesake and grandson of the legendary coach Viktor Tikhonov, made two goals. (Belyaev, "Sport. The Stadium," 2014)

Тихо́ня

A gentle, quiet, and shy person. Typically conveys disapproval or displeasure, but can also sound positive.

Derived from the adjective **ти́хий** *quiet*. Can be a synonym for **па́инька**.

See **па́инька**.

Но э́тот тихо́ня и скро́мник уме́л держа́ть класс лу́чше, не́жели ины́е гимнази́ческие тира́ны. (Ю. Наги́бин «Учи́тель слове́сности» 1977)	But that meek and modest little man knew how to hold his class in his grip harder than any of the classroom tyrants at the school. (Nagibin, *The Literature Teacher*, 1977)
Уж тако́й тихо́ня был, тако́й пай, в пять часо́в всегда́ до́ма, не пил, не кури́л. . . (М. Ро́щин «Спеши́те де́лать добро́» 1979)	He was such a wallflower, such a good little boy, always home at five, never drank, never smoked . . . (Roshchin, *Hurry Up and Do Good*, 1979)
Он был тако́й тихо́ня – никто́ пове́рить не мог, что он мо́жет соверши́ть не́что отча́янное.	He was such a quiet man – nobody could believe that he could do something reckless.
Не поня́тно, как послу́шный ребёнок и сми́рная тихо́ня могла́ преврати́ться в капри́зное и вре́дное существо́.	It's a mystery how a good little girl like that could turn into such a capricious and mischievous creature.

Entries 103

Транжи́ра

A wastrel. Someone who spends money carelessly, thoughtlessly, and ceaselessly. Can express displeasure, but at the same time can be sympathetic.

Derived from the verb **транжи́рить** *to splurge* and the noun **транжи́р** *spendthrift.* Synonymous with **мот** *wastrel.* Antonymous with **скря́га, сквалы́га.** Combined with the adjective **легкомы́сленный** *irresponsible* and is associated with **гуля́ка, кути́ла,** and **про́жига.**

See **гуля́ка, кути́ла, про́жига, скря́га, сквалы́га.**

Достое́вский был транжи́ра и бесконе́чно ще́дрый челове́к. (И. А́нненский «Кни́га отраже́ний» 1906)	Dostoevsky was a wastrel and an infinitely generous individual. (Annensky, *The Book of Reflections*, 1906)
И за всех плати́л Серафи́м Миха́йлович, челове́к не про́сто широ́кий, а настоя́щий транжи́ра. (Т. Шмы́га «Сча́стье мне улыба́лось. . .» 2000)	And Serafim Mikhailovich paid for everyone. He wasn't just a generous man – he was a real wastrel. (Shmyga, *Fortune Smiled at Me*, 2000)
Прики́нь, Во́ва, я бы уж давно́ был миллионе́ром, е́сли б не Ли́дка. Та ещё транжи́ра! (Т. Тро́нина «Руса́лка для инти́мных встреч» 2004)	Get this, Vova: I would have long ago been a millionaire if not for Lidka. And a high-roller! (Tronina, *A Mermaid for Intimate Get-Togethers*, 2004)
Она́ не была́ легкомы́сленной транжи́рой – про́сто не копи́ла де́ньги и с лёгкостью их тра́тила.	She wasn't an irresponsible wastrel – she simply stored up money and spent it easily.

Трудя́га

Used to refer to a person who works a lot. Expresses approval and generally positive emotions.

Derived from the noun **труд** *work, labor,* and verb **труди́ться** *to work, to labor.* Synonymous with **работя́га**[1] and antonymous with **лентя́юга.**

See **лентя́юга, работя́га**[1].

Всегда усердная, усидчивая
(пухлое надгубье выпячено),
самозабвенная трудяга.
(И. Грекова «Фазан» 1984)

Ever a dedicated, diligent
(puffy upper lip thrust out), and
selfless busy bee. (Grekova,
The Pheasant, 1984)

И Виктор прекрасный человек,
говорю я, умница, трудяга,
его последняя книга о русской
иконе четырнадцатого века
удивительна. (Д. Рубина
«Двойная фамилия» 1986)

And Viktor is a wonderful person,
I say, clever, hard-working, his
last book on Russian iconography
of the fourteenth century is
fascinating. (Rubina, *The Dual
Last Name*, 1986)

Умер Мордвинов – трудяга,
хороший актёр, никому
не улыбался и никого не
сжирал – жалею, плачу.
(А. Щеглов «Фаина
Раневская: Вся жизнь» 2003)

Mordvinov died – he was a hard
worker, a good actor, never
smiled at anyone and never
destroyed anyone – I regret it
and I cry.

Тупица

Someone who is extremely dimwitted. Articulates disdain and scorn.

Derived from the adjective **тупой** *dumb* and the noun **тупость** *stupidity*. Associated with **невежда** and **незнайка,** but expresses more negativity. Semantically close to **болван** *moron*. Synonymous with **бездарь** *mediocrity*.

See **невежда, незнайка**.

Я не тупица, не лопух,
понимал свою задачу, ценил
их помощь, старался, у них не
было оснований жаловаться
на меня. (А. Рыбаков
«Тяжёлый песок» 1978)

I'm not a numbskull or a
moron, I understood the job,
valued their help, and tried my
best – they had no reason to
complain about me. (Rybakov,
Heavy Sand, 1978)

«Челюсти» был аспирант,
заваливший три раза
подряд диалектический и
исторический материализмы
и, как безнадёжный тупица,

"Jaws" was a graduate student
who failed dialectical and
historical materialism three
times in a row and was kicked
out of the program as a

отчи́сленный из аспиранту́ры. (А. Солжени́цын «В кру́ге пе́рвом» 1968)

hopeless dimwit. (Solzhenitsyn, *In the First Circle*, 1968)

А Па́влов э́тот – безгра́мотный тупи́ца, пу́тает криминоло́гию с криминали́стикой, в сло́ве «перспекти́ва» по четы́ре оши́бки де́лает. (А. Мари́нина «Стече́ние обстоя́тельств» 1992)

That Pavlov is an illiterate nitwit who confuses criminology with forensics and makes four mistakes in the word "perspective" alone. (Marinina, *A Confluence of Events*, 1992)

О́льга – непроходи́мая тупи́ца, на́до объясня́ть элемента́рные ве́щи по не́скольку раз.

Olga is an unflappable dimwit; you have to explain elementary things to her several times.

Уби́йца

A murderer.

Derived from the verb **уби́ть** *to kill*. Its synonym **ки́ллер** *hitman* connotes a certain professionalism and fees. Used in combination with the adjective **сери́йный** *serial*.

В су́мраке во́дорослей колыха́лись солда́тиками Ге́рманн и Раско́льников – неча́янный уби́йца-дворяни́н с незаря́женным пистоле́том и злонаме́ренный уби́йца-разночи́нец с навострённым топоро́м. (Ю. Давы́дов «Си́ние тюльпа́ны» 1990)

In the shadows of the weeds rippled Hermann and Raskolnikov – the inadvertent murderer-nobleman with the unloaded gun and the malicious murderer-raznochinets with the sharpened axe. (Davydov, *Blue Tulips*, 1990)

Не зна́ю, пра́вда и́ли нет, бу́дто сосе́ди слы́шали иль в мили́ции уби́йца призна́лась, что Никола́й на мгнове́ние вы́рвался из её лап и успе́л сказа́ть: «Лю́да, я же тебя́ люблю́». (В. Аста́фьев «За́теси» // «Но́вый мир» 1999)

I don't know if it's true. Either the neighbors heard about it or else the murderer confessed to the police that Nikolai momentarily tore himself from her grasp and managed to say: "Lyuda, I love you." (Astafyev, "Notches," 1999)

106   *Entries*

У́мница

An informal expression used to praise people for some accomplishment or good behavior, regardless of their level of intelligence.

Derived from the adjective **у́мный** *smart*. **У́мница** is less informal than its synonyms **молодчи́на** and **молодча́га**.

See молодчи́на (молодча́га).

Ты зна́ешь, он фи́зик. Умопомрачи́тельная у́мница. (В. Аксёнов «Пора́, мой друг, пора́» 1963)	You know, he's a physicist. He's staggeringly on top of things. (Aksyonov, *It's Time, My Friend, It's Time*, 1963)
У нас на кварти́ре жил оди́н учёный – тако́й у́мница, тако́й башкови́тый, до́брый то́же тако́й. . . (В. Шукши́н «Пе́чки-ла́вочки» 1972)	A scientist lived in our apartment – he was such a clever man, quick on the update, kind too . . . (Shukshin, *Happy Go Lucky*, 1972)
Она́ одна́ расти́ла двух дете́й – его́ и Ната́шку, очарова́тельную весну́щатую девчу́шку, у́мницу, люби́вшую кни́ги. . . (Б. Ле́вин «Блужда́ющие огни́» 1995)	She raised two kids all by herself – him and Natashka, a charming girl with freckles who liked books . . . (Levin, *Wandering Fires*, 1995)
«У́мница!» – воскли́кнула Лю́ба, уви́дев, что Па́ша суме́л собра́ть весь стол, пока́ её не́ было.	"Well done!" cried Lyuba, seeing that Pasha managed to build the whole table while she was out.

Уро́дина

An ugly individual with physical defects and blemishes or with moral flaws. Articulates scorn and disdain.

Derived from the nouns **уро́д** *freak*, **уро́дство** *deformity* and the adjective **уро́дливый** *hideous*. The adjectives **мора́льный** *moral* and **нра́вственный** *moral* are combined with the noun to indicate a morally deficient person. The nouns **краса́вец** *pretty boy* and **краса́вица** *beauty* are antonyms.

Entries 107

Я ви́дел, как Бори́с, наду́в свои́ желваки́, потяну́л за ру́ку каку́ю-то худу́ю, некраси́вую же́нщину, соверше́нную уро́дину в плато́чке, и пошёл с ней танцева́ть. (Ю. Три́фонов «И́гры в су́мерках» 1970)

I saw how Boris, puffing out his cheeks, pulled up some skinny, unattractive woman in a scarf, horribly ugly, and went to dance with her. (Trifonov, *Games in the Twilight*, 1970)

По́мню, как ты всё врал: уро́дина, гу́бы то́лстые, нос криво́й. . . (В. Сиду́р «Па́мятник совреме́нному состоя́нию» 2002)

I remember how you kept lying: ugly, fat lips, crooked nose . . . (Sidur, *A Monument to the Modern Condition*, 2002)

В о́бщем, я, подро́сток-уро́дина, встреча́лась со взро́слым мужчи́ной-краса́вцем. (Т. Солома́тина «Мой оде́сский язы́к» 2011)

In short, I, an ugly teenager, was seeing a handsome grown-up man. (Solomatina, *My Odessan Language*, 2011)

Кака́я же я уро́дина – проти́вно в зе́ркало на себя́ смотре́ть.

I'm just so ugly – I can't even look in the mirror.

Ханжа́

A hypocritical prude who hides behind virtue and morals with regard to sex. Conveys disdain and condemnation.

Derived from the noun **ха́нжество** *sanctimony*. Semantically close to **лицеме́р** *hypocrite*, which focuses on hypocrisy in general, while its synonym **свято́ша** stresses one's hypocrisy vis-à-vis one's purported puritanism.

See **свято́ша**.

У ханжи́ в одно́м карма́не – де́ньги, в друго́м – моли́твенник, ханжа́ слу́жит и бо́гу и чёрту, обма́нывает и

A hypocrite has money in one pocket and a prayer book in the other, he serves both God and the Devil, lying to both one and

того и другого. (А. Макаренко «Книга для родителей» 1937)

the other. (Makarenko, *A Book for Parents*, 1937)

. . . в глазах ребят Тоня была лицемерка и ханжа, её прежние проповеди стоили так же мало, как теперешняя кротость. (В. Кетлинская «Мужество» 1938)

. . . in the eyes of the guys, Tonya was a hypocrite and a prude; her prior sermons were worth as little as her present humility. (Ketlinskaya, *Courage*, 1938)

Ребята, я не ханжа, я догадываюсь, откуда дети берутся, но должны же быть элементарные правила поведения в общественном месте! (А. Семёнов «Без правил» // «Знание – сила» 1998)

Guys, I'm not a prude, I can imagine where children come from, but there need to be basic rules of behavior in public places! (Semyonov, "No Rules," 1998)

Жуткий ханжа был этот Виталик. Потому что по молодости лет не успел нагрешить сам. (О. Некрасова «Платит последний» 2000)

Vitalik was a terrible hypocrite. Because he didn't get the chance to sin because of his age. (Nekrasova, *The Last One Pays*, 2000)

Ханыга

Someone whose position in life has sunk drastically and who often drinks himself into a stupor. Typically conveys strong condemnation and is used to refer to males. The diminutive **ханыжка** expresses more sympathy.

Derived from the verb **ханыжничать**, which conjures the image of someone drinking, someone whose position in life has sunk and who looks sloppy.

See the synonyms **забулдыга**, **пропойца**, **пьяница**.

Сторож был ханыга, обыкновенный алкаш и вдруг «Лимонная». (Э. Хруцкий «Осень в Сокольниках» 1983)

The guard was a down-on-his-luck drunk, an ordinary alcoholic, and then, suddenly, "Limonnaya" [a fancy vodka]. (Khrutsky, *Fall in the Sokolniky*, 1983)

Немно́го повора́чивает го́лову, а на сосе́днем холме́ копа́ется ханы́га, оде́тый во все дра́ное, не по ро́сту, я́вно с чужо́го плеча́. (А. Мото́ров «Преступле́ние до́ктора Парово́зова» 2013)

He turned his head slightly, and on the neighboring hill digging around was a drunk, wearing only torn things, not in his size, clearly someone else's. (Motorov, *Doctor Parovozov's Crime*, 2013)

По физионо́мии ви́дно, что э́тот тип ханы́га подворо́тный.

It's clear by his mug that he's an alley drunk.

Хапу́га

Someone who takes, grabs, accepts unlawfully, and takes bribes. Conveys strong contempt, disparagement.

Derived from the verb **ха́пать** *to nick*, which is colloquial. Semantically very close to **вор** *thief* and **ворю́га** and even closer to **стяжа́тель** *moneygrubber*, which focuses on saving money, and is often combined with these words.

See **ворю́га**.

Ещё в ма́е, когда́ приезжа́ли снима́ть, она́ не понра́вилась На́де – ме́сто невзра́чное, хозя́йка кака́я-то угрю́мая и хапу́га, три́ста пятьдеся́т за две ко́мнатки с вера́ндой. . . (Ю. Три́фонов «В грибну́ю о́сень» 1968)

Even in May, when they came to rent the apartment, Nadya didn't like it – the place was unattractive, the housewife was surly and moneygrubbing, three hundred and fifty for two small rooms with a porch . . . (Trifonov, *The Fungal Autumn*, 1968)

Друго́й коммуни́ст в на́шей кварти́ре был кудря́вый озорни́к, рестора́тор Федо́т Бойцо́в, вор и хапу́га, но он вы́летел из па́ртии, очи́стившей таки́м о́бразом свой ряды́ от его́ прису́тствия. (Ю. Наги́бин «Моя́ золота́я тёща» 1994)

The other communist in our apartment was a curly-haired mischief maker, thief, and moneygrubber, but he was kicked out of the party, which cleansed its ranks of his presence. (Nagibin, *My Precious Mother-in-Law*, 1994)

Ей посове́товали хоро́шего специали́ста и́менно по э́той ча́сти, назва́ли та́ксу, О́льга дёрнула плечо́м: «Хапу́га!» (Г. Щербако́ва «А́рмия любо́вников» 1997)	They recommended someone who specialized in it and named the price, at which Olga jerked her shoulder: "Leech!" (Shcherbakova, *An Army of Lovers*, 1997)

Хвастуни́шка

A boaster. Since it is a diminutive of **хвасту́н** *braggart*, it typically addresses children. Conveys disapproval, but can also be indulgent and condescending.

Also derived from the verb **хва́статься** *to brag*. Its synonym **бахва́л** *braggart* expresses more negativity, because it stresses one's self-assertion and is associated with arrogance. Can be associated with **вруни́шка** and **лгуни́шка**.

See **вруни́шка, лгуни́шка**.

От тако́го хвастуна́ и сын хвастуни́шка бу́дет! (В. Кетли́нская «Му́жество» 1938)	The son of a braggart like that will be a braggart himself! (Ketlinskaya, *Courage*, 1938)
Ах ты, хвастуни́шка несча́стный! «У меня́ в дере́вне кру́пных происше́ствий не быва́ет!» (В. Липа́тов «Дереве́нский детекти́в. Три зи́мних дня» 1968)	You wretched braggart! "Nothing exciting ever happens in my village!" (Lipatov, *A Village Murder Mystery. Three Winter Days*, 1968)
Ла́дно, всё вы́яснено: я очуме́лая от ме́лкого успе́ха хвастуни́шка, зазна́йка, наха́лка. . . (Ф. Кно́рре «Ка́менный вено́к» 1973)	Alright, alright, it's all clear now: I'm an insolent braggart and know-it-all who's gone mad from success . . . (Knorre, *The Stone Wreath*, 1973)
Како́й же Ва́ська хвастуни́шка и враль. Уже́ никто́ не ве́рит, когда́ говори́т пра́вду.	Vas'ka is such a braggart and fibber. Nobody believes him anymore, even when he tells the truth.

Entries 111

Хитрю́га

A very cunning and crafty person. Frequently refers to children, expressing playfulness.

Derived from the noun **хитре́ц** *clever boy* and the adjective **хи́трый** *cunning*, which articulates a more negative overtone. The noun **лиса́** *fox* and the adjective **ло́вкий** *deft* are associated with **хитрю́га**. Antonymous with **проста́к** *simpleton*.

Тогда́ Ма́шка, хитрю́га, протя́гивает ру́ку и бы́стро сдёргивает с отцо́вского но́са очки́. (А. Пантеле́ев «На́ша Ма́ша» 1966)

At which point Mashka, that clever girl, reaches out and swiftly yanks the glasses off of her father's nose. (Panteleev, *Our Masha*, 1966)

Ты почему́ обижа́ешь мла́дшего бра́та и ещё визжи́шь при э́том, хитрю́га! (В. Миха́льский «Прощёное воскресе́нье» // «Октя́брь» 2009)

Why are you bullying your younger brother and squealing the whole time, you sly devil! (Mikhal'sky, "The Forgiven Sunday," 2009)

Хитрю́га дя́дя Бо́ря не рассказа́л племя́ннику, куда́ они́ е́дут, и тот не по́нял, что они́ е́дут на рыба́лку, пока́ не уви́дел о́зеро.

Sly Uncle Borya didn't tell his nephew where they were going, and he didn't realize that they were going fishing until he saw the lake.

Ну что, хитрю́га, доби́лась своего́? Получи́ла карандаши́ – тепе́рь рису́й.

So, clever girl, happy now? You've got the crayons – now go draw something.

Худы́шка

Refers to someone who is thin, often children and especially girls. Articulates warm feelings and sympathy.

Derived from the adjective **худо́й** *thin*.

Из тёмного угла́ вы́скочила непоня́тного во́зраста худы́шка в джи́нсах и с

A skinny girl of ambiguous age wearing jeans jumped out of the dark corner and called out,

чайником в руке, крикнула: «Привет!» (О. Новикова «Женский роман» 1993)

"Hiya!" (Novikova, *A Woman's Novel*, 1993)

Да и я была в их годы худышка, – как должное принимая комплимент, сказала Мари. (В. Михальский «Река времён. Ave Maria» // «Октябрь» 2010)

"I was a skinny girl during those years too," said Marie, accepting the compliment as a matter of course. (Mikhalsky, "The River of Time. Ave Maria," 2010)

Какой же ты худышка! Просто жалко смотреть.

You're such a skinny boy! It's painful just to look at you.

Чертяка (чертяга)

Can express approval, praise, and admiration, as well as negative emotions towards someone.

Derived from the noun **чёрт** *fiend*. Combines with adjectives like **хитрый** *cunning* and **умный** *smart*. Can be synonymous with **умница** and **молодец** (a word used to convey the meaning of "good job"), which is typically used to express praise.

See **умница**.

Оба мальчика задохнулись от смеха, у Пети изо рта пошли даже пузыри. – Что ж ты брызгаешься, чертяка? (В. Катаев «Белеет парус одинокий» 1936)

Both boys were out of breath for laughter, spittle even started flying from Petya's mouth. "What're you spraying for, you little devil?" (Kataev, *A Lonely White Sail*, 1936)

Баба его, Бурсачка, любила певческий хор и взяла, чертяка, привычку ходить к обедне в собор. (В. Лихоносов «Ненаписанные воспоминания. Наш маленький Париж» 1983)

His woman, a seminarian, loved the choir and the devil developed the habit of going to the cathedral during Mass. (Likhonosov, *Unwritten Memoirs. Our Little Paris*, 1983)

Он обнял меня, попридержал в объятиях,

He hugged me, held me in his arms, patting my back,

похло́пывая руко́й по
спине́, и прошепта́л:
«Спаси́бо, чертя́ка!
Я слезу́ да́же пусти́л».
(Е. Ве́сник «Дарю́, что
по́мню» 1997)

and whispered: "Thanks, you
little devil! I even teared up
a bit." (Vesnik, *I Give What I
Remember*, 1997)

Ну чертя́ка! Молоде́ц Ксю́ха!
И до́ма всё успева́ет сде́лать,
и в институ́те всё у неё
хорошо́.

What a fiend! Well done,
Ksyukha! She gets everything
done at home, *and* her studies
are going great!

Чисти́юля

A person who is obsessed with cleanliness and hygiene. Often refers
to children. Can articulate either a positive or negative overtone.

Originates from the adjective **чи́стый** *clean* and the verb **чи́стить** *to
clean*. Can be used figuratively and be synonymous with **чистоплю́й
(чистоплю́йка)** *sissy* when the person seeks to avoid the unpleasant facets of life. In this case, it is semantically associated with
белору́чка. Antonymous with **грязну́ля, замара́шка,** and **неря́ха**.

See **белору́чка, грязну́ля, замара́шка, неря́ха**.

Чиха́ть она́ хоте́ла на э́ту
ве́чно мокрогу́бую ханжу́
и чистю́лю! (М. Шо́лохов
«По́днятая целина́» 1959)

She didn't give a damn about that
eternally wet-lipped hypocrite
and clean freak. (Sholokhov,
Virgin Soil Upturned, 1959)

Ишь ты, кака́я чистю́ля! –
вдруг со зло́бой ощери́лся
Лёвка. – Други́е пусть
ма́жутся, а я в стороне́
постою́, а? (Ю. Три́фонов
«Дом на на́бережной» 1976)

"Such a goody-goody!" Lyovka
suddenly snarled. "Let others
get dirty, while I stand off to
the side, right?" (Trifonov, *The
House on the Waterfront*, 1976)

Явля́лись они́ под ве́чер
всегда́ приоде́тыми, но
на откры́той вера́нде у
Симоно́вичей сиде́ли босы́ми,
так как Ве́ра Симоно́вич была́
чистю́ля и у неё, когда́ ни

They would arrive in the early
evening, always dressed up,
but they would sit barefoot
on the Simonoviches' porch,
since Vera Simonovich was a
clean freak, and her floors was

зайди́, свежевы́мытые полы́. (В. Пьецу́х «Ле́том в дере́вне» // «Но́вый мир» 2000)

Абсолю́тный поря́док, что и говори́ть, хозя́ин был изве́стный чистю́ля, да́же пусты́е буты́лки он скла́дывал в каки́е-то щеголева́тые я́щики, вы́крашенные под хохлому́. (Е. Су́хов «Де́лу коне́ц – сро́ку нача́ло» 2007)

spotless at any given time of day. (Pyetsukh, "In the Village in the Summer," 2000)

There was complete order – the owner was a renowned clean freak; he even put empty bottles into stylish-looking boxes painted to look like khokhloma. (Sukhov, *The Job Ends – The Term Begins*, 2007)

Чуди́ла

A strange individual. Someone who acts in a peculiar fashion. Expresses amazement. Stylistically neutral and can convey disapproval.

Originates from the noun **чу́до** *wonder* and the verb **чуди́ть** *behave oddly*. Synonymous with **чуда́к** *odd fellow*.

Ну и чуди́ла ты! Бормо́чешь что-то, а разобра́ть ничего́ нельзя́. (А. Но́виков-Прибо́й «Цуси́ма» 1932–1935)

You're such an odd fellow! You're constantly mumbling something, but you can't make anything out. (Novikov-Priboy, *Tsushima*, 1932–1935)

Му́ля мне вчера́ предлага́л съе́здить в Оста́нкино – там како́й-то музе́й дре́вностей («о́чень интере́сный») и «краси́вый парк». Вот чуди́ла! – Пра́вда, э́то он сове́тует от чи́стого се́рдца, но не мо́жет поня́ть, что мне соверше́нно ску́чно е́хать в Оста́нкино одному́! (Г. Эфро́н «Дневники́» 1940)

Mulya asked me yesterday if I wanted to go to Ostankino – there's some museum of ancient history there ("very interesting") and a "pretty park." What an odd guy! His recommendation is coming from a good place, but he just can't get that it's super boring for me to go to Ostankino by myself! (Efron, *Journals*, 1940)

А чего́ во́дку откры́л, пить сюда́ прие́хал? Ну чуди́ла ты. . . (М. Ве́ллер «Хочу́ в Пари́ж» 1990)

What did you open the vodka for? What, did you come here to drink? Weirdo . . . (Veller, *I Want to Go to Paris*, 1990)

| Никола́й Петро́вич тако́й чуди́ла, так стра́нно ведёт себя́. Всегда́ то́лько ди́ву даёшься. | Nikolai Petrovich is such an oddball, he acts so strange. You're always left in wonder. |

Шаромы́га

Someone who likes to lead a luxurious lifestyle on someone else's dime. Conveys strong negative emotions. Sounds scornful, disdainful, disparaging. Not used very often in contemporary language.

Synonymous with **шаромы́жник** *bum*, which sound less strong. Semantically close to **вы́жига, прощелы́га**, and **моше́нник** *swindler*.

See **вы́жига, прощелы́га**.

. . . он был уж на ле́стнице, как вдруг у са́мого его́ но́са, неизве́стно отку́да, вы́рос удиви́тельного разме́ра городово́й, а в уша́х пренеприя́тно зазвуча́ло: «А куда́ ты, шаромы́га, ле́зешь?» (М. Салтыко́в-Щедри́н «Неви́нные расска́зы. Запу́танное де́ло» 1848–1863)	. . . he was on the stairs when a policeman appeared out from under his very nose, and his ears were filled unpleasantly with the question: "And where are you going, you moocher?" (Saltykov-Shchedrin, *Innocent Stories. A Tangled Affair*, 1848–1863)
Што о́коло возо́в-то трёшься, шаромы́га ты э́дакая, полу́ночная? (А. Леви́тов «Беспеча́льный наро́д» 1869)	What are you doing idling next to the carts, you midnight moocher? (Levitov, *A Carefree People*, 1869)
Э́тот шаромы́га опя́ть попыта́лся вы́нести ку́чу проду́ктов со скла́да.	That moocher once again tried to walk out of the warehouse with a bunch of products.

Ше́льма

A cunning, dishonest swindler. Conveys negative emotions, but can also be tinged with admiration.

The verb **шельмова́ть** *defame* originated from **ше́льма**. **Моше́нник** *swindler*, **плут** *scoundrel*, and **пройдо́ха** are synonymous, though the latter has the connotation of "experienced". Associated with

116   *Entries*

the adjective **ло́вкий** *deft*, **хи́трый** *cunning*. The expression **бог шельму́ ме́тит** *God marks the crook* and the adjectives **краси́в/ краси́вая** *pretty*, **хоро́ш/хороша́** *good* are widely used in phrases with **ше́льма** in discourse.

See **пройдо́ха**.

. . . ла́зил по чужи́м сада́м и бахча́м, вся шко́ла, все учителя́ и преподава́тели от него́ сто́ном стона́ли, не было дня без дра́ки, без разби́того но́са, без подби́того гла́за. И хи́трый, ше́льма! (А. Рыбако́в «Тяжёлый песо́к» 1978)

. . . he trespassed in gardens and melon fields. The whole school, all the teachers were miserable because of him – not a day went by without a fight, a broken nose, a black eye. And he was clever, the scoundrel! (Rybakov, *Heavy Sand*, 1978)

Ведь он, ше́льма, прегениа́льнейшая бе́стия, э́тот Са́шка! (Ю. Безеля́нский «В сада́х любви́» 1993)

That Sashka is a swindler, an insolent beast! (Bezelyansky, *In the Gardens of Love*, 1993)

К нам он приезжа́л па́ру раз, всю́ду ходи́л, всё выню́хивал, иска́л упуще́ния, но ше́льма Гу́щин ло́вко обводи́л гра́фа вокру́г па́льца и да́же получи́л за отли́чную слу́жбу табаке́рку. (М. Ши́шкин «Всех ожида́ет одна́ ночь» 1993)

He visited us a couple of times, wandered around, sniffing everything out, searching for oversights, but the rogue, Gushchin, cunningly led the count on a merry chase and was even rewarded with a snuffbox for outstanding service. (Shishkin, *The Same Night Waits for Everyone*, 1993)

Оста́вь её. Что ей, ше́льме, сде́лается. Сама́ кого́ хо́чешь проведёт.

Leave her alone. A crook like her will be fine. She herself can wind whomever she wants around her finger.

Я́беда

A snitch. Someone who reports things about others. Often refers to children. Conveys strong disapproval and disdain.

Entries 117

Derived from the noun **я́бедник** *snitch* and the verb **я́бедничать** *to snitch*. Associated with the adjective **трусли́вый** *cowardly*.

Я не я́беда, я пе́ред все́ми говорю́: Се́ня плохо́й челове́к. – Вы представля́ете, ещё говори́т, что не я́беда! (А. Дра́бкина «Волше́бные я́блоки» 1975)

"I'm not a snitch, I'm saying in front of everyone that Senya is a bad person." "You hear that! And yet he still says he's not a snitch!" (Drabkina, *Magic Apples*, 1975)

Ты тако́й сме́лый и че́стный, а дружи́л с нехоро́шей де́вочкой, с кото́рой никому́ не сле́дует дружи́ть! Она́ – я́беда! Доно́счик! (В. Железнико́в «Чу́чело» 1981)

You're so brave and honest, and yet you were friends with a bad girl that no one should be friends with! She's a snitch! An informant! (Zheleznikov, *The Scarecrow*, 1981)

Я́беда Кароли́на бе́гает к дире́ктору чуть ли ни ка́ждый день жа́ловаться на всех и на всё.

That snitch, Carolina, runs to the director almost every day to complain about everyone and everything.

Bibliography

Абрамов Ф. "Братья и сёстры", Москва: "Советский писатель", 1982.

Азольский А. "Диверсант" // "Новый мир", 2002, №3–4.

Акимов В. "Плата за страх", Москва: Вагриус, 2000.

Аксёнов В. "Апельсины из Марокко", Москва: Эксмо, 2006.

Аксёнов В. "Новый сладостный стиль", Москва: Эксмо, 1997.

Аксёнов В. "Пора, мой друг, пора", Москва: "Молодая гвардия",1963.

Аксёнов В. "Таинственная страсть. Роман о шестидесятниках", Москва: "Семь Дней", 2009.

Алданов М. "Ключ", Париж: YMCA-Press, 1950.

Алексеев Г. "Зелёные берега", 1990, http://orel.rsl.ru.

Амфитеатров А. "Марья Лусьева", Москва: НПК "Интелвак", 2000.

Андреев Л. "Жертва", 1916, www.leonidandreev.ru/povesti/zhertva.

Анненский И. "Вторая книга отражений". Москва: "Наука", 1979.

Анненский И. "Книга отражений", Москва: "Наука", 1979.

Антонов С. "Разноцветные камешки" // "Огонёк", 1959, №15.

Арбузов А. "Годы странствий" 1954. www.theatrestudio.ru/library/catalog. php?author=arbuzov

Архипова И. "Музыка жизни", Москва: Вагриус, 1998.

Астафьев В. "Затеси" // "Новый мир", 1999, №8.

Астафьев В. "Последний поклон"/"Собрание сочинений". В 15-ти томах. Т.5, Красноярск, "Офсет", 1997.

Астафьев В. "Прокляты и убиты", Москва: Эксмо, 2007.

Астафьев В. "Царь-рыба"/"Царь-рыба: Повествование в рассказах", Москва: "Современник", 1982.

Афиногенов А. "А внизу была земля", Москва: "Советская Россия", 1982.

Бабель И. "Баграт-Оглы и глаза его быка"/"Конармия", Москва: "Правда", 1990.

Баконина М. "Девять граммов пластита", Москва: Вагриус, 2000.

Bibliography 119

Безелянский Ю. "В садах любви", Москва: Вагриус, 2002.

Белых Г., Пантелеев А. "Республика ШКИД", Ленинград: "Детская литература", 1986.

Беляев А. "Человек-амфибия", Москва: "Детская литература", 2001.

Беляев А. "Спорт. Стадион" // "Огонёк", 2014, №19.

Белоусова В. "Второй выстрел", Москва: Вагриус, 2000.

Бенуа А. "Жизнь художника". Нью-Йорк: Издательство им. Чехова, 1955.

Берсенева А. "Возраст третьей любви", Москва: Эксмо, 2005.

Берсенева А. "Полет над разлукой", Москва: Эксмо, 2005.

Благов С. "Улыбка Анахиты" // "Юность", 1971, №1.

Бондаренко В. "Подаяние грешного Глебушки . . ." // "Наш современник", 2003, №12.

Бояшов И. "Танкист или "Белый тигр", Москва: "Лимбус Пресс", 2008.

Браво А. "Комендантский час для ласточек" // "Сибирские огни", 2012, №7.

Брагинский Э., Рязанов Э. "Тихие омуты", Москва: АСТ, Зебра Е, 2000.

Буйда Ю. "Город палачей" // "Знамя", 2003, №2/3.

Буйда Ю. "Рассказы о любви" // "Новый мир", 1999, №11.

Булгаков М. "Мастер и Маргарита"/Избранная проза, Москва: "Художественная литература", 1966.

Варенцов Н. "Слышанное. Виденное. Передуманное. Пережитое", Москва: "Новое литературное обозрение", 2011.

Васильев Б. "Были и небыли", Москва: Вагриус, 1999.

Васильев Б. "Оглянись на середине" // "Октябрь", 2003, №6.

Вахтин Б. "Гибель Джонстауна", Ленинград: "Советский писатель", 1986.

Веллер М. "Карьера в Никуда", 1988, http://modernlib.ru/books/demidov_ georgiy/lyudi_gibnut_za_metall/read/.

Веллер М. "Хочу в Париж", Москва: Вагриус, 1997.

Вертинская Л. "Синяя птица любви", Москва: Вагриус, 2004.

Весник Е. "Дарю, что помню", Москва: Вагриус, 1997.

Волков О. "Погружение во тьму", Москва: Вагриус, 2001.

Волконский С. "Мои воспоминания", Москва: "Искусство", 1992.

Воронель Н. "Без прикрас. Воспоминания", Москва: "Захаров", 2003.

Воронский А. "Гоголь", Москва: "Молодая гвардия", 1934.

Гайдар А. "Пусть светит", Москва: "Правда", 1986.

Гаршин В. "Заметки о художественных выставках" 1887, http://az.lib. ru/g/garshin_w_m/text_0240.shtml.

Гейнце Н. "Дочь Великого Петра", Смоленск: "Русич", 1913.

Геласимов А. "Фокс Малдер похож на свинью: Повесть, рассказы", Москва: ОГИ, 2001.

120   *Bibliography*

Герман Ю. "Дорогой мой человек", Москва: "Правда", 1990.

Герман Ю. "Россия молодая", Ленинград: "Советский писатель", 1954.

Гиппиус З. "Без талисмана"/Собрание сочинений, Москва: "Русская книга", 2001.

Гладилин А. "Большой беговой день", Москва: Вагриус, 2001.

Голицын С. "Записки уцелевшего" Москва: "Орбита", 1990.

Горланова Н. "Что-то хорошее", Москва: Вагриус, 2000.

Горький М. "Жизнь Клима Самгина". Собрание сочинений в 30-ти т. Т. 20. Москва: ГИХЛ, 1953.

Гранин Д. "Искатели", Ленинград: Лениздат, 1979.

Гранин Д. "Месяц вверх ногами". Собрание сочинений в 6-ти томах. Т.4. Москва: "Художественная литература", 1979.

Грачев А. "Ярый-3. Ордер на смерть", Москва: Вагриус, 2000.

Грачев А. "Ярый против видеопиратов", Москва: Вагриус, 1999.

Грекова И. "Перелом"/"На испытаниях", Москва: "Советский писатель", 1990.

Грекова И. "Под фонарём"/"На испытаниях", Москва: "Советский писатель", 1990.

Грекова И. "Фазан", Москва: "Советский писатель", 1984.

Григорьев С. "Александр Суворов", Москва: "Детская литература", 1988.

Громов В. "Компромат для олигарха", Москва: Вагриус, 2000.

Гроссман В. "Всё течёт" // "Октябрь", 1989, №6.

Гроссман В. "Жизнь и судьба", Москва: Книжная палата, 1992.

Гурченко Л. "Аплодисменты" 1994–2003, Москва: Вагриус, 2004.

Давыдов Ю. "Синие тюльпаны", Москва: Вагриус, 1997.

Дворецкий Л. "Шакалы", Москва: Вагриус, 2000.

Демидов Г. "Люди гибнут за металл", 1972–1980, http://modernlib.ru/ books/demidov_georgiy/lyudi_gibnut_za_metall/read/.

Довлатов С. "Армейские письма к отцу"/"Сергей Довлатов: творчество, личность, судьба (итоги Первой международной конференции "Довлатовские чтения", Санкт-Петербург: "Звезда", 1999.

Довлатов С. "Иная жизнь"/Собрание прозы. В 3-х томах. Т.2, Санкт-Петербург: Лимбус-пресс, 1984.

Довлатов С. "Наши", Энн-Арбор: Ардис, 1983.

Домбровский Ю. "Факультет ненужных вещей", Москва: "Художественная литература", 1989.

Домбровский Ю. "Хранитель древностей"/Собрание сочинений в 6-ти томах. Т.4, Москва: Терра, 1992.

Достоевская А. "Воспоминания", Москва: "Захаров", 2002.

Достоевский Ф. "Бесы", Ленинград: "Наука", 1972.

Достоевский Ф. "Господин Прохárчин", 1846, https://ilibrary.ru/text/20/ index.html.

Достоевский Ф. "Дневник писателя" // "Гражданин", 1872, №34.

Достоевский Ф. "Село Степанчиково и его обитатели", 1859, https://ilibrary.ru/text/60/index.html.

Драбкина А. "Волшебные яблоки", Ленинград: "Детская литература", 1975.

Дубов Н. "Небо с овчинку", Москва: "Детская литература", 1966.

Евсеев Б. "Евстигней" // "Октябрь", 2010, №5.

Евтушенко Е. "Волчий паспорт", Москва: Вагриус, 1999.

Ерофеев В. "Москва-Петушки", Москва: Вагриус, 2001.

Ерофеев В. "Моя маленькая лениниана"/Собрание сочинений. В 2-х томах. Т.2, Москва: Вагриус, 2001.

Ефимов Б. "Десять десятилетий", Москва: Вагриус, 2000.

Железников В. "Каждый мечтает о собаке", Москва: "Детская литература", 1985.

Железников В. "Чучело", Москва: "Детская литература", 1985.

Жемайтис С. "Большая лагуна", 1977, www.litmir.me/br/?b=30947&p=1.

Жжёнов Г. "Прожитое", Москва: Вагриус, 2002.

Залыгин С. "Комиссия", 1976, http://modernlib.ru/books/zaligin_sergey/komissiya/.

Звягин Е. "Всемирная паутина" // "Звезда", 2002, №5.

Зосимкина М. "Ты проснёшься", Монреаль: Accent Graphics Communications, 2015.

Зощенко М. "Перед восходом солнца", Москва: Вагриус, 2004.

Иванова Т. "Портрет моего мужа" // "Семейный доктор", 2002, №10.

Измайлов Л. "Аферисты", 1996, http://rulibs.com/ru_zar/humor_prose/izmaylov/0/j32.html

Иличевский А. "Перс: Роман", Москва: АСТ, 2010.

Иоффе, Г. "Общество было утомлено. История "Выборгского воззвания" // "Наука и жизнь", 2006, №6.

Искандер Ф. "Гнилая интеллигенция и аферизмы" // "Знамя", 2001, №11.

Искандер Ф. "Письмо"/"Стоянка человека", Москва: СП Квадрат, 1995.

Искандер Ф. "Поэт" // "Новый мир", 1998, №4.

Искандер Ф. "Сандро из Чегема". Москва: "Московский рабочий", 1989.

Кабаков А. "Масло, запятая, холст", Москва: Вагриус, 2000.

Кабо Л. "Ровесники Октября", 1997, http://lit.lib.ru/k/kabo_l_r/rovesniki.shtml.

Казаков Р. "Отцовский инстинкт" // "Семейный доктор", 2002, №5.

Капица С. "Мои воспоминания", Москва: "Российская политическая энциклопедия", 2008.

Каралис Д. "Автопортрет", Санкт-Петербург: Геликон Плюс, 1999.

122 *Bibliography*

Каралис Д. "Космонавт" // "Нева", 2002.

Карамзин Н. "Волшебный фонарь или картина Парижа" // "Вестник Европы", 1802, №19.

Кара-Мурза С. "Антисоветский проект", Москва: "Алгоритм", 2002.

Карапетян Д. "Владимир Высоцкий: Воспоминания", Москва: "Захаров", 2002.

Катаев В. "Белеет парус одинокий", Москва: Эксмо, 2007.

Катаев В. "Юношеский роман", 1983, www.litmir.me/br/?b=13712&p=1.

Кетлинская В. "Мужество", Москва: ГИХЛ, 1957.

Ким А. "Белка. Роман-сказка", Москва: "Советский писатель", 1984.

Кнорре Ф. "Каменный венок", Москва: "Художественная литература", 1984.

Кожевников В. "Щит и меч", Москва: "Советский писатель", 1968.

Кожевникова Н. "В лёгком жанре"/"Гарантия успеха", Москва: "Аграф", 2004.

Кожевникова Н. "Шура и Настенька"/Москва: "Аграф", 2004.

Козаков М. "Актёрская книга", Москва: "Вагриус", 1998.

Козинцев Г. "Тут начинается уже не хронология, но эпоха . . ."/"Время трагедий", Москва: Вагриус, 2003.

Колмогоров А. "Мне доставшееся: Семейные хроники Надежды Лухмановой", Москва: Аграф, 2013.

Колышкин В. "Тайна сэра Моррисона" // "Вокруг света", 1997.

Короленко В. "Письма" 1889. Собрание сочинений в 10-ти т. Т. 10. Москва: ГИХЛ, 1956.

Крюков Т. "Стражи порядка" // "Наука и жизнь", 2008, №2.

Кузмин М. "Дневник 1934 года", Санкт-Петербург: Издательство Ивана Лимбаха, 1998.

Куприн А. "Гранатовый браслет"/Собрание сочинений. В 9-ти томах. Т.5, Москва: "Художественная литература", 1972.

Куприн А. "На переломе", 1957, https://ilibrary.ru/text/1757/p.1/index.html.

Куприн А. "Олеся"/Собрание сочинений. В 9-ти томах. Т.2, Москва: "Художественная литература", 1971.

Кучерская М. "Современный патерик: чтение для впавших в уныние", Москва: "Время", 2004.

Кучерская М. "Тётя Мотя" // "Знáмя", 2012, №7–8.

Лавренев Б. "Крушение республики Итль", Москва: "Правда", 1990.

Ларина А. "Незабываемое", Москва: Вагриус, 2002.

Левин Б. "Блуждающие огни", Москва: Захаров, 2002.

Левитов А. "Беспечальный народ", Москва: "Художественная литература", 1977.

Леонов Л. "Лекарство от жизни", Москва: Эксмо, 2001.

Bibliography 123

Леонов Л. "Русский лес", Москва: "Художественная литература", 1953.

Лимонов Э. "Молодой негодяй"/Собрание сочинений. В 3-х томах. Т.1, Москва: Вагриус, 1998.

Лимонов Э. "Подросток Савенко", Москва: Вагриус, 1998.

Липатов В. "Деревенский детектив. Три зимних дня", Москва: "Молодая гвардия", 1983.

Лиснянская И. "Величина и функция" // Москва: "Знамя", 1999, №7.

Лихоносов В. "Ненаписанные воспоминания. Наш маленький Париж", Москва: "Советский писатель", 1987.

Личутин В. "Вдова Нюра"/Повести, Москва: "Известия", 1981.

Маканин В. "Андеграунд, или герой нашего времени", Москва: Вагриус, 1999.

Макаренко А. "Книга для родителей", Москва: "Правда", 1971.

Маринина А. "Стечение обстоятельств", Москва: Эксмо, 2005.

Матвеева Л. "Продлёнка", Москва: "Детская литература", 1987.

Медведев Р. "Андрей Сахаров и Александр Солженицын", Москва: "Права человека", 2002.

Мережковский Д. "Воскресшие Боги. Леонардо да Винчи"/Собрание сочинений. В 4-х томах. Т.1. Москва: "Правда", 1990.

Михальский В. "Одинокому везде пустыня", Москва: "Согласие", 2003.

Михальский В. "Прощёное воскресенье" // "Октябрь", 2009, №1.

Михальский В. "Река времён. Ave Maria" // "Октябрь", 2010, №7.

Можаев Б. "Саня"/"Живой", Москва: "Советская Россия", 1977.

Молчанов В. "Дорогие страницы памяти" // "Наш современник", 2004, №6.

Моторов А. "Преступление доктора Паровозова", Москва: АСТ, 2014.

Мстиславский С. "Грач – птица весенняя", 1937, http://2lib.ru/book/win/14371.xhtmll.

Нагибин Ю. "В те юные годы"/"Утраченная музыка", Москва: "Подкова", 1998.

Нагибин Ю. "Дневник", Москва: "Книжный сад", 1996.

Нагибин Ю. "Рассказы о Гагарине", 1979, http://lib.rus.ec/b/280493/read.

Нагибин Ю. "Учитель словесности", Кишинев: "Литература артистикэ", 1985.

Найман А. "Все и каждый" // "Октябрь", 2003, №1.

Найман А. "Славный конец бесславных поколений", Москва: Вагриус, 1999.

Некрасова О. "Платит последний", Москва: Вагриус, 2000.

Николаева Г. "Битва в пути", Москва: "Советский писатель", 1960.

Новикова О. "Женский роман"/"Мужской роман. Женский роман", Москва: Вагриус, 2000.

124 Bibliography

Новиков-Прибой А. "Цусима", 1932, www.e-lib.info/download. php?id=1120000302.

Новицкая В. "Безмятежные годы", 1912, http://az.lib.ru/.

"Парк культуры" // "Столица", 1997, №19.

Носов С. "Фигурные скобки", Санкт-Петербург: Лимбус-пресс, 2015

Окуджава Б. "Путешествие дилетантов", Москва: "Современник", 1990.

Окуневская Т. "Татьянин день", Москва: Вагриус, 1998.

Орлов В. "Альтист Данилов", Москва: "Советский писатель", 1981.

Осипович-Новодворский А. "Карьера", Санкт-Петербург: "Наука", 2005.

Павлов О. "Казённая сказка", Москва: Вагриус, 1999.

Панова В. "Серёжа"/Собрание сочинений. В 5-ти томах. Т.3, Ленинград: "Художественная литература", 1987.

Пантелеев А. "Наша Маша: Книга для родителей" // Собрание сочинений. В 4-х томах. Т.4, Ленинград: "Детская литература", 1984.

Пастернак Б. "Доктор Живаго", Москва: "Художественная литература", 1990.

Пелевин В. "Любовь к трём цукербринам", Москва: Эксмо, 2014.

Пелевин В. "S.N.U.F.F.", Москва: Эксмо, 2011.

Петросян М. "Дом, в котором . . .", Москва: "Гаятри", 2009.

Петрушевская Л. "Маленькая волшебница" // "Октябрь", 1996, №1.

Пивоварова И. "Мечта Кости Палкина"/"Однажды Катя с Манечкой", Москва: "Детская литература", 1986.

Пильняк Б. "Три брата", www.magister.msk.ru/library/prose/pilnb005.htm.

Писемский А. "Люди сороковых годов", Москва: "Правда", 1959.

Писемский А. "Русские лгуны", Москва: "Правда", 1959.

Платонов А. "Течение времени", Москва: "Московский рабочий", 1971.

Полянская И. "Прохождение тени", Москва: Вагриус, 1999.

Постников В. "Карандаш и Самоделкин в стране людоедов", Москва: "Рипол-классик", 1997.

Постников В. "Шапка-невидимка", Москва: "Рипол-классик", 1997.

Приставкин А. "Вагончик мой дальний" // "Октябрь", 2005, №8.

Пропп В. "Исторические корни волшебной сказки", Ленинград: Издательство Ленинградского университета, 1986.

Пьецух В. "Летом в деревне" // "Новый мир", 2000, №6.

Ремизов В. "Воля вольная" // "Новый мир", 2013, №11–12.

Рецептер В. "Узлов, или обращение к Казанове"/"Ностальгия по Японии", Москва: Вагриус, 2001.

Розов В. "Удивление перед жизнью", Москва: Вагриус, 2000.

Ростовский А. "По законам волчьей стаи", Москва: Вагриус, 2000.

Bibliography 125

Рощин М. "Спешите делать добро", Москва: "Советский писатель", 1984.

Рубина Д. "Белая голубка Кордовы", Москва: Эксмо, 2009.

Рубина Д. "Двойная фамилия", Москва: Вагриус, 2002.

Рубина Д. "Медная шкатулка", Москва: Эксмо, 2015.

Рубина Д. "Русская канарейка. Блудный сын", Москва: Эксмо, 2015.

Рыбаков А. "Тяжёлый песок", Москва: Советский писатель, 1982.

Рязанов Э. "Подведённые итоги", Москва: Вагриус, 2000.

Савельев А. "Аркан для букмекера", 2000, http://litlife.club/br/?b=248098&p=41

Садур Н. "Немец", Москва: Вагриус, 2000.

Салтыков-Щедрин М. "Невинные рассказы/Запутанное дело", Москва: "Художественная литература", 1965.

Салтыков-Щедрин М. "Пёстрые письма", Москва: "Художественная литература", 1966.

Сапегина В. "Ещё раз о Бунине" // "Сибирские огни", 2012, №3.

Санаев П. "Похороните меня за плинтусом" // "Октябрь", 1996, №7.

Семёнова А. "Без правил" // "Знание-сила", 1998, № 3.

Сергеев-Ценский С. "Недра". Собрание сочинений в 12-ти томах. Т.2, Москва: "Правда", 1967.

Сидур В. "Памятник современному состоянию", Москва: Вагриус, 2002.

Симонов К. "Так называемая личная жизнь", Москва: "Художественная литература", 1982.

Синицына В. "Муза и генерал", Москва: Вагриус, 2002.

Сиркес П. "Труба исхода", Москва: РИФ РОЙ, 1999.

Слаповский А. "Висельник"/"День денег", Москва: Вагриус, 2000.

Слаповский А. "Синдром феникса" // "Знамя", 2006, №11–12.

Смехов В. "Театр моей памяти". Москва: Вагриус, 2001.

Снегирёв А. "Вера", Москва: Эксмо, 2015.

Снегирёв А. "Зимние праздники" // "Знамя", 2012, №3.

Солженицын А. "В круге первом" // "Новый мир", 1990.

Соловейчик С. "Ватага "Семь ветров", Москва: "Детская литература", 1979.

Соломатина Т. "Мой одесский язык" Москва: Эксмо, 2011.

Солоухин В. "Смех за левым плечом: Книга прозы", 1989, http://gosudarstvo.voskres.ru/solouhin/leftsh.

Спивакова С. "Не всё", Москва: "Вагриус", 2002.

Сухов Е. "Делу конец – сроку начало", Москва: Эксмо, 2007.

Станюкович К. "Вокруг света на Коршуне", Москва: "Государственное издательство географической литературы", 1953.

Стрелкова И. "Похищение из провинциального музея"/"Одна лошадиная сила: Повести", Москва: "Детская литература", 1984.

126　*Bibliography*

Толстой Л. "Юность"/Собрание сочинений, Москва: "Художественная литература", 1958.

Трауб М. "Семёновы"/"Домик на юге", Москва: АСТ, 2009.

Трифонов Ю. "В грибную осень", Москва: "Художественная литература", 1987.

Трифонов Ю. "Другая жизнь"/Собрание сочинений в 4-х томах. Т.2. Москва: "Художественная литература", 1986.

Трифонов Ю. "Игры в сумерках", Москва: Эксмо, 2008.

Трифонов Ю. "Нетерпение"/Собрание сочинений в 4-х томах. Т.3. Москва: "Художественная литература", 1986.

Трифонов Ю. "Победитель"/"Дом на набережной", Москва: Эксмо, 2008.

Трифонов Ю. "Предварительные итоги", Москва: "Художественная литература", 1978.

Трифонов Ю. "Старик"/Избранное, Минск: Вышэйшая школа, 1983.

Трифонов Ю. "Утоление жажды", Москва: "Советский писатель", 1970.

Тронина Т. "Никогда не говори "навсегда", Москва: Эксмо, 2004.

Тронина Т. "Русалка для интимных встреч", Москва: Эксмо, 2004.

Тургенев И. "Дворянское гнездо"/Собрание сочинений, Москва: "Наука", 1954.

Тургенев И. "Конец Чертопха́нова", 1872, https://ilibrary.ru/text/1204/p.22/index.html.

Тургенев И. "Хорь и Калиныч"/"Записки охотника", Москва: "Детская литература", 2000.

Тынянов Ю. "Пушкин", Ленинград: "Художественная литература", 1974.

Тэффи Н. "Брошечка", Москва: "Художественная литература", 1990.

Успенский М. "Там, где нас нет", Санкт-Петербург: "Азбука", 2002.

Фрумкина Р. "О нас – наискосок", Москва: "Русские словари", 1997.

Хазанов Б. "Похож на человека"/"Город и сны", Москва: Вагриус, 2001.

Хруцкий Э. "Осень в Сокольниках", Москва: Московская ассоциация писателей-криминалистов, Интербук, 1991.

Цветаева М. "Мои службы", 1919, http://lib.ru/POEZIQ/CWETAEWA/sluzhby.txt.

Чарская Л. "Приютки", Приход храма сошествия Святаго Духа, "Русская миссия", 2007.

Чарушин Е. "Тюпа, Томка и сорока", Москва: ООО "Книги "Искателя", 2004.

Чехов А. "Воры"/Полное собрание сочинений и писем, Москва: "Наука", 1974.

Чехов А. "Горе"/Полное собрание сочинений и писем, Москва: "Наука", 1974.

Bibliography   127

Чехов А. "Свадьба"/Полное собрание сочинений и писем, Москва: "Наука", 1974.

Членов А. "Как Алёшка жил на Севере", Москва: "Детская литература", 1965.

Чуковская Л. "Прочерк", Москва: "Время", 2009.

Чуковская Л. "Сочинения". В 2-х томах. Т.1, Москва: "Гудьял-Пресс", 2000.

Чуковский К. "Серебряный герб", Москва: "Детская литература", 1985.

Чулаки М. "Примус" // "Звезда", 2002, №1–2.

Шахиджанян В. "1001 вопрос про ЭТО", Москва: Вагриус, 1999.

Шварц Е. "Обыкновенное чудо"/"Пьесы", Ленинград: "Советский писатель", 1972.

Шварц Е. "Снежная королева", Ленинград: "Советский писатель", 1972.

Шимадина М. "Игра по правилам и без" // "Эксперт", 2013, №4.

Шишкин М. "Венерин волос" // "Знамя", 2005, №4.

Шишкин М. "Всех ожидает одна ночь", Москва: Вагриус, 2001.

Шишкин М. "Письмовник" // "Знамя", 2010, №7.

Шишков В. "Емельян Пугачев: Историческое повествование", Москва: "Правда", 1985.

Шмелёв И. "Лето Господне", 1927–1944, www.lib.ru.

Шмелёв И. "Солнце мёртвых", Москва: "Согласие", 2000.

Шмыга Т. "Счастье мне улыбалось", Москва: Вагриус, 2001.

Шолохов М. "Поднятая целина", Москва: Государственное издательство художественной литературы, 1960.

Шолохов М. "Тихий Дон", Москва: "Молодая гвардия", 1980.

Шпанов Н. "Ученик чародея", Москва: "Воениздат", 1956.

Шукшин В. "Печки-лавочки", Москва: Вагриус, 2003.

Шукшин В. "Хахаль", Москва: Вагриус, 2003.

Щеглов А. "Фаина Раневская: Вся жизнь", Москва: "Захаров", 2003.

Щёголев А. "Чёрная сторона зеркала"/"Новогодний Дозор: Лучшая фантастика", Москва: АСТ, 2014.

Щербакова Г. "Ангел Мёртвого озера" // "Новый мир", 2002, №7.

Щербакова Г. "Армия любовников", Москва: Вагриус, 2001.

Щербакова Г. "Ах, Маня . . ."/"Год Алены", Москва: Вагриус, 2002.

Щербакова Г. "Год Алёны", Москва: Вагриус, 2002.

Щербакова Г. "Мальчик и девочка", Москва: Вагриус, 2001.

Эпштейн М. "Ленин-Сталин" // "Родник", 1989, №6.

Эренбург И. "Оттепель", Москва: "Советский писатель", 1956.

Эфрон Г. "Дневники", Москва: Вагриус, 2004.

Юрский С. "Чернов"/"Содержимое ящика", Москва: Вагриус, 1998.

Яковлев А. "Омут памяти". В 2-х томах. Т.1, Москва: Вагриус, 2001.

List of Russian nouns of common gender

аферю́га 1

балабо́лка 2
бедня́га (бедня́жка, бедня́жечка) 2
бедола́га 3
белору́чка 3
бродя́га (бродя́жка) 4
брюзга́ 5

вообража́ла 6
ворю́га 7
вражи́на 7
вре́дина 8
вруни́шка 9
всезна́йка 9
вы́жига 10
выпива́ла 11
выпиво́ха 12
вы́скочка 12

горемы́ка 13
грязну́ля 14
гулёна 14
гуля́ка 15

деля́га 16
доходя́га 17
дури́ла 18

егоза́ 18
ехи́дина 19

жа́дина (жадю́га) 20

забия́ка 21
забулды́га 21
заводи́ла 22
задава́ка (задава́ла) 23
зади́ра 24
зазна́йка 24
за́йка 25
замара́шка 26
запева́ла 27
зану́да 27
зева́ка 28
злю́ка (злю́чка) 29
зубри́ла (зубри́лка) 30

кале́ка 30
кана́лья 31
капризу́ля 32
книгоно́ша 33
колле́га 34
копу́ша 34
короты́шка 35
кривля́ка 36
кровопи́йца 37
кро́ха 38
кро́шка 38
кути́ла 39

ла́комка 40
ла́пушка 41

List of Russian nouns of common gender 129

лгуни́шка 41
лежебо́ка 42
лентя́юга 43
ловчи́ла 44
лома́ка 44

мази́ла[1] 45
мази́ла[2] 46
малю́тка 47
маля́вка 47
миля́га 48
молодчи́на
   (молодча́га) 49
мудри́ла 50
мя́мля 50

невéжа 51
невéжда 52
невиди́мка 52
недотёпа 53
недотро́га 54
недоу́чка 55
нéженка 56
незна́йка 57
непосéда 58
неро́вня 58
неря́ха 59
неумéйка 60
неумéха (неумёха) 61
ню́ня 62

обжо́ра 63
объеда́ла 63
одино́чка 64

па́инька 65
писáка 66
плáкса 66
побиру́шка 67
подли́за 68
подлипáла 69
подлю́ка (подлю́га) 69
подпевáла[1] 70
подпевáла[2] 71
попрошáйка 71

почему́чка 72
привере́да 73
придира 73
прилипáла 74
приставáла 75
про́жига 75
пройдо́ха 76
пролáза 77
проны́ра 78
пропо́йца 79
простофи́ля 79
прощелы́га 80
пустомéля 81
пья́ница 82
пьянчу́га
   (пьянчу́жка) 82

работя́га[1] 83
работя́га[2] 84
раззя́ва 85
рази́ня 86
размазня́ 87
растя́па 87
растеря́ха 88
растрёпа 89
рёва 90
ро́вня 90
ро́хля 91

самоу́чка 92
свято́ша 93
симпатя́га 93
сквалы́га 94
скря́га 95
скромня́га 96
сладкое́жка 97
сластёна 98
со́ня 98
стиля́га 99
сутя́га 100

тарато́рка 100
тёзка 101
тихо́ня 102
транжи́ра 103

130 *List of Russian nouns of common gender*

трудя́га 103
тупи́ца 104

уби́йца 105
у́мница 106
уро́дина 106

ханжа́ 107
ханы́га 108
хапу́га 109
хвастуни́шка 110

хитрю́га 111
худы́шка 111

чертя́ка (чертя́га) 112
чистю́ля 113
чуди́ла 114

шаромы́га 115
ше́льма 115

я́беда 116